Run Sally Run

Run Sally Run

My Childhood as an
Identical Twin

by Sally Bair

Cedar Haven Books
Washburn, Wisconsin

Run Sally Run

Published by
Cedar Haven Books
P.O. Box 186
Washburn, Wisconsin 54891-0186

First edition   ISBN 978-0-9841346-3-2

For Sandy
my other half

CONTENTS

Introduction

My story includes facts, foibles, and funnies about my identical twin sister and me, about our symbiotic connection from before birth until we separated after our high-school graduation. I call those formative years the "we" years because our lives in the "we" meant companionship and comfort, support and survival. Oneness.

Since this is a compilation of *my* stories as well as *our* stories, I confess to taking literary liberty in some of them. After all, though we looked and acted alike, we viewed people and events differently. I give my twin the liberty to disagree with a few of my stories. Only a few, mind you.

I began daily journal writing in 1963, not during our young years of the 1940s as I wish I had. My love of *writing* words came long after *reading* them. The simple stories about Dick and Jane and Sally and Spot and Puff gave me a love for reading that stays with me today.

My sister and I, both goal-oriented and highly competitive, rushed to see who could spell the most words correctly and who could read the most books. In fact, we spent our first seventeen years rushing to get ahead—and stay ahead—of each other. Our lives became a race to be first, best, smartest, bravest, and strongest.

When I talk about running, I don't mean relays, sprints, or long-distance races that could have made me a genuine athlete. I mean my race through life. The race that would put me ahead of my twin.

I usually won our races. But not always.

Run, Sally, Run Hot and Cold

The summer of 1936 is recorded as the hottest in U.S. history. Minnesota, the state of my birth, also holds that record. The only saving grace of the "Great Heat Wave" and the prolonged national drought was the low humidity. For days on end, temperatures reached over one hundred degrees across the entire country and including in Minneapolis, our home town.

My mom Ruth Bunker Christiansen, pregnant with me and my twin that summer, along with my dad Edwin Christiansen, joined people everywhere spreading blankets on the lawns and sleeping there each night when the temperatures dropped into the low nineties. One day in July when Minneapolis registered 108 degrees, the St. Paul Daily News want-ad staff ordered 400 pounds of ice and two electric fans to cool the air in the press room. Housewives also used ice, twenty-five-pound blocks of it, delivered by ice trucks that traveled up and down the city streets to sell their precious product. Ice was in high demand—a hot commodity—to fill our ice boxes in a day when there was no electric refrigeration.

The winter of '36, by contrast, held record low temperatures. We were born on December 14, one of those extremely cold days.

My twin and I have been competitive our whole lives. It might have started in the womb. I fought to be first and hit the ground running—my first race. I must have kicked her, because she didn't come around for another forty-five minutes. For a mother in labor, that's a long time. While I dried off, suckled my first meal, and enjoyed the new world, my twin struggled to keep up. And so the pattern began. She spent her whole life trying to catch me.

Back then, new mothers were required to remain in their hospital beds for ten days. Mom's first time out of bed came when she was released from Deaconess Hospital. A nurse helped her into a wheelchair and placed a baby in each arm. Her doctor came in to see "the only identical twins I've ever delivered," and then had to catch us before we fell from Mom's arms as she fainted from weakness.

We didn't receive our names for days. On our birth certificates, we're called Twin A and Twin B. Daddy wanted to name us after two of his French girlfriends he'd met during his time spent fighting the Germans in France. Mom would have nothing to do with that. She named me Sally Ann—Ann after Daddy's mother named Anna. Sandra Lee was named after Mom's mother named Leila. That settled the affair.

I called Sandra San. Mom called her Sandy.

Although Mom and Daddy (we never called him Dad) didn't attend any church, Mom had us baptized in the Lutheran faith since it happened to be the church of Daddy's Norwegian family. Because of the severe cold, Mom asked the pastor to baptize us at home. She didn't dare risk taking us out. Daddy's old, black Chevrolet didn't have a good heater so he used it only for work and, of course, to take him to the tavern and back home.

Both of us weighed a hefty six pounds each, give or take a few ounces. We grew quickly and by summer our arms and legs were a mass of pudgy creases. Our sister, Donna Joan (we called her Jo), was almost nine years older and held the dubious chore of having to babysit at times. In the beginning, she was enamored by her identical baby sisters and enjoyed wheeling us around the block in Mom's white wicker buggy during our first summer. We sat facing each other, the buggy's sun shield curving around whichever one of us happened to sit in the back, as Jo pushed the buggy along the narrow sidewalk.

Jo wheeled us home one hot day, indignant. "Mom, a neighbor lady came over to see the twins," she said. "She saw their heat rash and gave me a dirty look. She told me to make you take better care of them."

Because the hot spell lasted through 1937, we had developed heat rash in the fat creases of our arms and legs. Mom must have used a case of talcum powder that summer to help keep the ugly, prickly rash away from our bodies.

Our parents bought a house that summer near our rented one, a small house tucked between two others in the middle of the block of 41st Avenue South in Minneapolis.

San and I weren't the only twins in our neighborhood. At each end of the street across from us lived a pair of twin boys. One block away lived a set of identical triplets. It was common to see one set of twins, Nile and Lyle, AKA Jeepie and Bussie, riding up and down the sidewalk on their trikes. Or the twin babies at the other corner of our block sharing a blanket in the warm sunshine. Or San and me perfecting cartwheels with Jean, Joan, and Jane in the front yard. Besides all of them, we had many other neighborhood friends who made our childhood days frolicking fun.

Most often, none of us could tell the other sets apart, dressed as we always were in identical outfits. The only difference in San and my clothing was the socks we wore. Mom dressed her in blue socks and me in red so she could more easily identify us. It was easier than checking San's crooked ear every time.

Dressing San and me alike was a matter of necessity for Mom. Living in a working class neighborhood such as ours demanded thrift. And Daddy's gambling meant she had little money to spend. Mom finagled a way to use less dress fabric than the patterns called for, thereby saving money on our clothes. She even made our underwear from remnants she bought at Kickernicks lingerie factory downtown.

Like most identical twins, we received a lot of attention. Being shy to the point of hiding behind Mom's dress when a stranger approached, we didn't *like* the attention. Mom probably became sick of hearing the question, "How do you tell which one is which?" Or, "Are they twins?" Some neighbors called us "Twinnie" because of their confusion. I always hated that name.

But Mom seldom mistook San from me. She usually used San's left ear as her marker, the one that didn't quite fold down at its tip like her other ear and like mine. Mom used that defect throughout our childhood except for one time, which perhaps happened during the night, when she accidentally bottle-fed one of us twice. My guess is I was the one who benefited, since I spent much of my life racing after food.

With growth and time, Mom began to notice differences between us. "Sometimes I forgot you were twins," she told us one time. She knew our physical attributes may have been similar, but our manners and interests became our own. At least, they did so in her estimation.

For instance, Mom discovered San had a strong determination in reaching for a bouncing ball Mom placed between us when we were babies. San stretched and grunted and fell flat on her belly until she grabbed the ball between her pudgy fingers. While she struggled to creep across the floor, I sat and watched her and then took off without effort, once again winning the race.

We shared an upstairs crib for sleep and a blanket spread on the living room floor for play. We shared a secret language of baby talk, too, which made Mom jealous. But Mom always treated us with love and care.

Like the day I fell down the front cement steps and cut my chin on a sharp stone. Mom threw off her apron, plunked us down into our shared red wagon, and pulled us to Dr. Belzer's residential office three blocks away. Dr. Belzer, the same doc who had delivered us two years earlier, commanded his nurse and Mom to hold me down while he stitched my wound and I screamed. After he slapped a bandage on me, San insisted she too needed a "garbage." Thus, we perpetuated our twinness, making it no less difficult for anyone to tell us apart.

See Sally Play

According to Mom, we slept and played in the crib we shared. And we wore flannel diapers, which Mom had to rinse out several times a day because she owned only two dozen. She dried them on the outside clothesline except on severely cold days; otherwise she hung them over a line in the basement. The cost of diaper flannel back in '36 topped at pennies per yard, but Mom had too little money to spend on more flannel.

Jo had to babysit occasionally and would rather have played with one of her visiting friends. As toddlers, we feared the dark. Jo took advantage of our fear, lining the doorway with white feathers—taken from her pillow, no doubt— and told us if we stepped on them the bogie man would get us. We didn't dare leave the room and clung to our fear of feathers for many years.

When we reached our third year, Mom saw to it we had a tricycle—to share. We rode double, up and down the sidewalk. Being the strongest twin, I usually pedaled while San stood behind me on the stepping bar. Mom's boundaries for us kept us from venturing across the street or alley. She had an easy time of enforcing them, since we were so shy and afraid of anything new, dark, or scary looking. Even the claws on the feet of our old-fashioned bathtub scared us. And of course feathers and the dark. We never went alone upstairs to our bedroom or to the only bathroom. Always two of us. Forever the two of us.

We played quietly in the house because Daddy worked nights and slept during the day. Mom kept us quiet by reading to us. She read before our naps and bedtime, teaching us the alphabet before we entered half-day Kindergarten. Our favorite stories included *The Wizard of Oz* series. We also enjoyed *Snip, Snap, Snurr, and the Gingerbread,* a newly-popular book about three boys as alike as identical triplets, who fell into a vat of gingerbread batter at a bakery and became gingerbread boys. A beautiful princess rescued them and took them to her palace, where they changed back into plain Swedish boys after a hard brushing and a bath.

With Mom nearby, we weren't afraid to play hide-and-seek under our dining room table, drape blankets around it for playing with our dolls inside, and sometimes use the upright, Eureka vacuum cleaner hoses for added play. The smell of dust that clung to its cloth bag lingered in my mind for years.

When Mom wasn't busy in the kitchen, sometimes she sat on the floor by the hot air vent, holding her forehead and crying from sinus pain. She told me later that one trip to a chiropractor cured her of that malady. Her crying also might have come from the stress of living with a husband who drank and gambled and controlled the money he earned.

Daddy paid little attention to his twin girls. According to big sister Jo years later, Daddy gave her lots of attention, like taking her fishing and playing board games with her. When Mom became pregnant with us, however, he bragged to his bar buddies about the son he expected. How disappointed and humiliated he must have felt when he became saddled with two more girls.

Mom more than made up for his inattentiveness. She kept us as safe and happy as a puppy with its new owner. Even without outward affection toward us, we knew she loved us. But we couldn't have been easy to care for. With little money to spend, Mom was forced to have us share our birthday cakes, our set of building blocks, our train and farm sets, our trike and wagon, and much more.

Oh! Oh! Sally is Sick!

"I don't feel good," I told Mom one day.

"You mean well," Mom corrected, as red bumps appeared on my face and neck.

"I don't feel good," San repeated two hours later.

"Well," came another correction.

We shared the measles, the mumps, chicken pox, another strain of measles, the flu, and colds. Mom took over our education during the "sick year" between our ages of six and seven. She didn't quit reading to us until we could read the books by ourselves. She read endlessly and tutored us so we could keep up with our school work. We missed half a year of first grade, but with her constant help, we didn't fall behind. The early reader books about Dick and Jane and Sally and Spot started us on a lifetime love for reading. Mom could hardly satisfy our new appetite for stories.

One disease we didn't share was encephalitis, which I contracted during the summer of my seventh year. With no antibiotics available back then, my recovery came from around-the-clock vigilance by Mom. During the days of that severe sleeping sickness, caused by an inflammation of the brain, I slept on a cot near the kitchen door so she could tend to me. Her diligent care and prayers to God brought total healing. San probably sat on the floor next to me playing with her toys, puzzled why I wouldn't stay awake.

San was my best friend. My confidante. My identity. And I hers. Wherever we went, we went together. Whatever we did, we did together. Whether pulling our wagon, riding our tricycle, playing dolls or jacks or cards, studying, or reading for pleasure, no one ever saw us apart. And we knew we looked alike. In fact, we looked so identical that our childhood photos sometimes confuse us today. Daddy, ever the quiet one of the household, rarely called us by name. He no doubt could not tell us apart.

Who is Sally? Who?

Visits from relatives, including yearly visits from Mom's parents, helped lighten Mom's heavy load. While Grandma Leila Bunker visited Mom, Grandpa Everett spent most of his time playing with us twins. He taught us how to say the alphabet backwards, how to play cards, and he joined us in playing with our cardboard farm set.

But Grandpa couldn't tell us apart. Every year it was the same. He'd ask one of us, "Which one are you?"

"I'm Sally. She's Sandy," I'd say.

"How can you tell each other apart?"

We'd laugh, give him a silly answer, and go on with our play.

According to Mom, one time when we were about three, San gave him a surprising answer. "Sal's wearing red socks and I'm wearing blue."

Grandpa asked, "What if you both wore red socks? Then how could you tell?"

San thought for a moment. "Then I guess we couldn't."

Grandpa had started to exhibit signs of Alzheimer's disease. Without being told about his memory loss, we seemed to recognize it and tolerated it, for we loved him and never tried to fool him about our identities.

And too shy to fool others, we fooled them by default. The day we brought our second-grade lessons home from school, Mom questioned why my marks had dropped for no apparent reason. She asked us, "Can your teacher tell you apart?"

"I think so," San said.

Curious, Mom asked her, "What does she call you? Sandy or Sandra?"

"She calls me Sally."

Shortly after, Mom made a trip to school for a talk with our teacher. When it came to defending us, she was like a she-bear protecting her young. And because of her constant dedication about our welfare, life treated us well, in spite of being poor. After all, we had each other. We had no need for much else. We shared everything—even our fear of the dark and of birds.

And we shared the same thoughts. When playing dolls, our thoughts wandered. One of us said, "Isn't she nice?" The other answered, "She sure is." Puzzled, Mom asked how we knew each other's thoughts. How could we explain our twinness? It was simply a part of us. We considered ourselves more like one person than two. Except when it came to food.

See Sally Eat

Ever the one who had to be first in line and always hungry, food became an ongoing obsession. One evening during our sixth year, while in the kitchen dressed in our nightgowns, I begged Mom for a peanut butter sandwich.

"No!" Mom kept repeating. "I'm busy making your lunches for tomorrow."

I kept begging. I whined. I cried.

Finally, out of exasperation, she told Jo, "Oh, just give her one and shove it down her throat."

The devil's gleam in her eyes, Jo grabbed a knife, filled it with creamy peanut butter, slapped it on a slice of Mom's homemade white bread, and shoved it into my throat while she held me in a vise grip. Between my frantic "mm-mmph" and "mmm-mmmph!" Mom managed to stop her from causing my demise. Of all substances to choke on, peanut butter rates as one of the worst.

But that incident didn't stop me from begging for food whenever I felt hungry. We may have lacked many things in our household, but never food. Daddy may have drunk and gambled his earnings away so we had few new clothes or toys, but he made sure we had enough to eat.

Mom kept a tiny garden behind our house so we enjoyed fresh vegetables during the summers. On warm, sunny days San and I ran barefoot between the rows to pick fresh peas and a carrot or two. A picket fence separated our property from our neighbors'. Some days we heard Mr. Walman cutting wood in his garage. We rarely saw his wife, but he often talked to us over the fence. Because of our extreme shyness, we were afraid of him.

About that time Mom took us on a train trip to Sawyer, North Dakota, to visit some of her cousins. She had spent her first fourteen years there and knew most everyone in the small town.

It was our first train ride. We walked up and down and up and down the aisle, intrigued by the train's rocking motion and clickety-clack of the wheels going down the tracks. We played games, counted trees, and amazed the man who sat behind us with our quick response to his arithmetic questions. He tried to teach us a bit of algebra, which befuddled us.

Once arriving, we stayed overnight at a cousin's farm. The alkaline water made us sick, so Mom had her hands full making frequent trips to the outhouse with us, keeping the bedbugs away from us, and trying to visit with her relatives. The kitchen smelled like sour milk and garbage. It held a big bucket called a slop pail, which was occasionally—but not often enough—emptied into the pigpen. We didn't eat much during that visit.

Outside stood a tall windmill with a water pump below. The bare yard buzzed with the cackling of chickens and geese, snorts of pigs, neighs of horses—and the incessant buzzing of flies. Since chickens wear feathers, we spent little time outside once we felt better. Besides, the wind blew most of the time. We did enjoy one of the second or third cousins who rode bareback on her horse for our benefit. Agile and talented, she rode the animal standing up on its back. She impressed us but we still remained inside.

The wide open spaces surprised me and made me lonesome for trees. I always did love trees, and wondered if that's why Grandpa and Grandma spent their later years in the forested, northwest part of Wisconsin.

See Sally at Home

Our own small backyard became a haven for us. We played in the sprinkler on hot days with neighborhood friends and pinned blankets along the clothesline to use as tents for playing dolls. For hours we dressed and undressed our dolls, pretending to feed them from our toy dishes, all the while wiggling and squirming on the grass that tickled our legs and bottoms. Back then all of us girls wore dresses, as shorts didn't come into style for several years.

On warm days we played on our open, front porch. The wooden floor had to be swept, as it often became littered with pine needles from the neighbor's Norway pine. We rocked our dollies on the metal swing or crouched on the floor where we devised elaborate doll houses from empty boxes, or played paper dolls. When we ran across the floor, our footsteps echoed from the open area below.

Our yard became a playground of flowers. Mom showed us how to make dolls from the hollyhock blossoms. We picked the thick, smooth leaves from her sedum plants, pressed down carefully to separate their membranes, and blew on them until they expanded into "frog bellies." We pushed our noses right into the lilac blossoms on our tall bush that grew on the narrow side of our house. We inhaled the heady fragrance of her tea roses blooming by the front sidewalk and picked handfuls of Lilies of the Valley for Mom. How we loved our gardens!

Some days we dared enter the small garage where Daddy kept his car in winter. He had been an auto mechanic before their marriage and had taken good care of his car and kept plenty of tools on his workbench and along the walls. After marrying Mom, he began working as a janitor-engineer for the Minneapolis School Board.

One tiny, high garage window shed just enough light so we could see where things lay. We inhaled the pungent odor of axle grease and motor oil but we never stayed long, fearing not only the dark, but bats and birds and creepy crawly things that set our imaginations running amok.

Daddy heated our house with coal, calling for delivery each fall. The truck tipped a load at a time through the one south window of the basement. The strong odor tickled my nose. Coal dust blew everywhere in the house through the air vents. One swipe of a finger along the wainscoting came up black as ... coal. Mom's job cleaning wasn't easy, but she shared the inconvenience with other wives.

Mom also cleaned up many puddles. Oh, we potty-trained early, and we didn't have a dog. But whenever the iceman delivered his 25-pound block of ice for our back porch icebox, chips flew everywhere, leaving little round puddles for little bare feet to find and track throughout the house.

The iceman's appearance meant that a host of neighborhood kids joined us in following him from house to house, hoping to snatch chips of ice that scattered our way when he dug his wicked looking tongs into a block of ice. Ah, the cooling taste of a misshapen ice cube on a hot, summer day! When a good lick or two didn't cool us fast enough, we bit down hard and chewed until the suddenness of a headache had us clutching the sides of our head as if we'd been hit with a baseball—but worth the effort.

Sometimes our running escapades were nipped in the bud by Mom's call.

"Sally! Sandy! Come practice your piano lessons."

Dragging our feet, we trudged up the street and into the house where we took turns practicing our scales.

Play Music, Sally, Play

I have always referred to our old upright piano as feminine. She needed tuning. As if that's all she needed. Three black keys—C sharp and F sharp on the second treble octave, and B flat on the lower end of the bass—had little sound. Two white keys also gave off a soft vibration. Worst of all, middle C was out of tune, even to our unsophisticated ears. We didn't care. We stretched our fingers up and down the keys, intent on winning another race.

The piano's name intrigued us. Squinting at its worn brand name above the keys, I spelled out the ornate letters. C-h-i-c-a-g-o. "CHICK-a-go," I shouted. Ever after, our piano became CHICK-a-go, even when we learned the proper pronunciation of the word Chicago. I named her Chick.

Our teacher had been a school teacher in her younger years. Old as she was, or at least seemed to us, she kept her strictness. Her skinny neck supported a little head with its tight-lipped face and perpetual frown. She walked with a cane. During her year-long tenure with us, she grimaced more than any teacher we'd ever seen. Not that we were such bad pupils. We learned the scales and how to play every song in John W. Thompson's Book I and Book II. But Chick's dull-sounding keys, eclipsed by her bad tuning, sent our teacher into fits of shaking and covering her ears. In fact, as the year wore on, her patience nearly wore out. Each week brought more frowns, more ear-coverings, more sighs. To her credit and to Mom's surprise, she persevered.

She persevered long enough to help us succeed in playing a duet for a piano recital she held. For the occasion, Mom sewed identical dresses of pale blue organza for us. Fabric back then cost about three yards for a dollar, so with more begging to Daddy, Mom bought, cut, and sewed the shimmery fabric.

The day arrived. Nervous as two cats in a cage, yet proud, we took the stage and finished our duet to the applause of the small audience.

The piece, called *In the Cradle,* was a tinkley tune filled with delicate fugues. I played bass while San played treble as we sat together on the piano bench, dressed in our fancy, baby blue dresses.

As we learned new songs during our seventh year, San and I began to enjoy music. We experienced the joy of a rhythmic, harmonious tune whether it came to our hungry ears as a soothing yet discordant lullaby, a rip-roaring march, or an emotional classic.

But on many days we groaned at Chick's inconsistencies, her sudden moods sparked by quiet keys. We begged Mom, without success, to hire a piano tuner. Daddy's night job with the School Board was secure during those Depression years, but between his gambling and drinking, we had little money to spend on such an extravagance as piano tuning. Chick remained in her defective state, but we loved her whether practicing our lessons or playing for fun. All along, however, we had to play quietly so Daddy could sleep.

Daddy sometimes came home half-drunk and belligerent, demanding a hot meal long after we had eaten, demanding we quit playing because his head hurt. During the frequent times when the tension of our parents' quarreling carried over to the supper table, we tried to tune out the ugliness with imaginary, new tunes to play on Chick the next day.

Chick's handicaps made us see with new eyes how joyful the music in one's heart can transcend the biggest, ugliest, most discordant sound. Middle C, the all-important key on a piano, could be out of tune. But all around it were other keys that brought harmony and happiness to us as we listened with our hearts.

See Sally Visit

Summertime during the WWII years brought many changes to our country. With the Depression waning, we now faced such things as food and gasoline rationing. Since Daddy had to drive to his place of work, he received more than enough coupons than needed—enough for us to take an occasional trip compared with many other people. We sometimes drove across Minneapolis to the city of Mound, located on Lake Minnetonka, where Daddy's brother, Henry, lived with his wife and five children. Grace, two or three years older than San and I, played with us near the weedy shore of the lake. They lived in the country at the top of a long hill in a big, white house. With no neighbors nearby and their house set far back from the busy lake road, it was always quiet.

We spent lots of time in their tiny parlor, which held a small organ that fascinated us and an ornately carved piece of furniture upon which sat an armadillo basket. The dried armadillo shell, with its tail curved into a handle, held odds and ends.

Uncle Henry owned an auto repair shop combined with a Phillips 66 gas station a mile or so down the highway. Daddy spent time there with his brother. That is, if they weren't drinking beer in the tool shed. They did their imbibing on the sly, since Aunt Emma was against drinking.

We spent time with our quiet cousin Grace, and Mom helped Aunt Emma in the kitchen. The only animals they kept were chickens. Of course, San and I *never* went near the chicken house.

Our favorite visit was to Range, Wisconsin, seventy miles away where Mom's parents, the Bunkers, lived. While Mom spent time with her parents, Daddy drove a few miles away to visit his sisters at their farm. We also visited them for a day. Daddy's oldest sister, Hattie, lived on a big farm with lots of chickens running around the yard. So San and I usually stayed indoors. No chickens for us. Unlike Grandma's plain home cooking, Aunt Hattie always spread a feast for us. She cooked delicious, Norwegian dishes and was known for her tasty desserts.

Some visits we didn't like were the ones we took with our parents to the local bar. Mom often went with Daddy to make sure he wouldn't get too drunk. She couldn't afford a baby-sitter on nights Jo, a teenager, went out on her own, so she took us along. Some nights we sat in the car and waited while they enjoyed their beer inside. In the winter we grew cold and complained, so after that they took us inside with them. We twins became a hit with everyone around and the other men teased Daddy about siring two kids at a time. All the while, we squirmed in our crowded corner of a booth, trying not to cough from the thick smoke, trying not to gag on the strong odor of beer. We hated those nights.

But we did enjoy our visits to our Victory Garden in the wartime summer.

See Sally Hoe

"We're going to the Victory Garden, kids," Mom called to San and me one hot, July day. "It's time to pick green beans and cucumbers again."

We were seven years old that summer of 1944 and the U.S. had been battling the Germans and Japanese for three years. Our government urged households to "Plant a Victory Garden—Help Feed our Servicemen!"

San and I threw our jump ropes onto the backyard sidewalk and ran into the house to grab our sweaters to keep us from being chilled in case of rain. At the back porch, we plucked our toy spades and rakes off the bottom shelf. We loved working in the garden soil.

Our Victory Garden lay at the edge of south Minneapolis past the airport. Daddy drove us there in our black Chevy. San and I enjoyed the ride because we had changed from shorts into overalls, which meant we wouldn't feel the scratchy horsehair of the back seat on our legs. We rode with the windows down and sang and counted telephone poles along the way. Twice we drove past Burma Shave signs:

Train approaching
Whistle squealing
Stop
Avoid that
Run-down feeling
Burma-Shave

The wolf
Is shaved
So neat
And trim
Red Riding Hood
Is chasing him
Burma-Shave

Daddy finally stopped the car at the garden and San and I piled out, toting a small basket containing four tin cups and, wrapped in newspapers, two Mason jars of Watkins orange nectar. We had to have something to quench our thirst while picking vegetables and hoeing during the hot hours. Our parents carried their garden tools and two bushel baskets.

The garden was huge. Several families shared the country plot. Our section lay in neat rows along the roadside edge, each row straight as a ruler. Previously, we'd already spent many hours helping Mom and Daddy hoe and pull weeds from the smooth soil.

"Let's go find the pumpkins," San said, pulling me down a long, long row. We skipped in single file, holding our arms straight out to our sides to feel the tallest leaves tickle our bare skin. At the end of the row, she stooped to uncover a light-orange pumpkin.

"Here's another one!" I yelled, startling a flock of grackles. They flew up in a whirr of wings from neighboring rows.

We checked under each vine and leaf, looking for pumpkins that might be ripe, wanting to hurry their growth. But they had to turn deeper orange before we could pick them in the fall.

We walked along the other garden rows, laughing as we squished our bare toes into the warm, moist soil. We checked each vegetable intently. Ran our fingers along silky Swiss chard leaves. Separated scratchy tomato vines. Peered under prickly cucumber leaves. Picked and opened plump peapods, popping the warm peas into our mouths. We played hide and seek between cornstalks and picked up garden bugs with our fingertips.

"Kids! Come and help pick green beans now," Mom called from the other end of our Victory Garden.

We skipped back to her and helped carry a bushel basket to the beginning of our two long rows of beans. The basket was already heavy with beet greens, Swiss chard, peas, and cucumbers that our parents had picked. Daddy walked to the other end of the rows with the other basket and bent over the bean vines there.

San, Mom, and I leaned over to separate thick, green bean leaves. No beans! We checked and rechecked, all the way down the row where we met Daddy in the middle. He looked at Mom. She looked at him.

Daddy's brow furrowed. "Someone stole all our green beans," he said.

Like wilted leaves, we slumped with discouragement.

Mom declared, "That's the last time we plant a Victory Garden, World War II or not."

Skate, Sally, Skate

As we grew older, our big sis Jo tolerated us more than she had before we started school. When we reached age nine, she took us by streetcar to Lake Nokomis a time or two to play on the beach while she lay sunning herself. But the day she took us roller skating eclipsed everything she'd ever done for us. I could even forgive her for earlier scaring us with feathers.

On the Sunday afternoon of her 17th birthday, she led us to the streetcar line where we rode with her to the roller rink on Lake Street. We sat on the streetcar's hard bench called the peanut row. She let both of us pull the trolley's cord so the conductor knew where to stop. From there we walked down Lake Street to the rink.

Jo had taken special care for the event. We had watched her dress in navy slacks and a soft, pink cashmere sweater. We peeked over her shoulder as she sat in front of her dressing table mirror and colored her eyelashes with black mascara to match her long hair, and smoothed a line of glowing red lipstick across each lip. The night before, she had filed her nails—fingers

49

and toes—and then painted matching red polish on them. How we longed to be like her, so beautiful and popular, so unafraid and talkative with boys. We dreamed and yearned for such glamor and social ease.

When we arrived at the long, wooden building with its domed roof of silver, we danced with anticipation ... and fear. Organ music floated all around, mingling with the deafening roar of wooden skate wheels rolling across the hardwood floor. Skaters laughed and shouted, whirled and fell. We watched and listened, in awe of the noise and activity.

Jo seemed to know many of the skaters. A fun-loving girl, she chatted and laughed while outfitting us with the white, shoe skates she had rented. We knew how to skate, having done so in our neighborhood along the sidewalks. But our skates were the clamp-on type with a key to tighten the clamps around our shoes. Nothing like the fancy ones we found ourselves wearing that day.

Jo guided us onto the rink, each of us clinging to a hand, until we became used to skating and could manage on our own—now clinging to each other for support.

Suddenly the organ began to play Happy Birthday and Jo's friends joined in singing to her. A boyfriend, tall and dark, skated over to her, embraced her in a romantic hug and bent her low into a long kiss. We watched in amazement. We'd never seen anyone kiss that way except in the movies.

The organ melted into a soft waltz and the announcer told us it was now "Couples Skate." Two of Jo's friends skated over to us, bowed, and each took one of us by the hand. My heart dropped to the pit of my stomach and my tongue turned ash-dry. I felt a blooming blush move up my face. My tall, handsome partner took my left hand in his left, my right hand in his right. He skated me around and around the room, smooth as a satin pillow, backwards and forwards, circling and spiraling till I became dizzy. But the dizziness came from the intense excitement of being in a boy's arms, dancing with grown-up skates in an indoor roller rink.

The way home brought us back to stark reality. We had to walk to the streetcar line in the dark, unsafe area along Lake Street. The streetcar, also dark as tar, took us to within two blocks from home. We jumped off and ran for home, again clutching Jo's hands. But our fear was eclipsed by the feelings of romance and speed and accomplishment we experienced at the roller rink.

Jo thrived on romance and fun. Known as a party girl, she sometimes entertained her friends at our house. I'm surprised Daddy allowed it, but she and he held a special bond. San and I sat on the top step of our stairway, dressed in our pajamas, to watch and listen. Too young to understand what they talked about, we still enjoyed the camaraderie obvious in the group. We especially enjoyed hearing Jo play Boogie-Woogie for her guests on our out-of-tune piano. Our eyes must have had stars in them as we dreamed of being as popular, as beautiful and talented and glamorous as our big sis, Jo.

One time she took us to a movie playing in a theater on Minnehaha Avenue. We walked there in the daylight and back home in the dark. The 25-cent movie terrified us. A murder mystery, it portrayed a young woman running from a villain, taking cover under a bed. She lay there, listening to the villain's footsteps drawing nearer and nearer then looked next to her where a skeleton lay. She screamed, of course. How it ended we don't know, as we had already tucked our legs under us in fear of a dead body beneath, and closed our eyes.

The walk home became a marathon with Jo again holding our hands. How did she manage to walk, let alone run, with us clinging to her body? Streetlights lit each intersection, but darkness lurked between. Every shadow, every shrub became a villain. Every swish of the breeze sounded like the rustle of the villain's silky shirt sleeves. We had nightmares about the movie for a long time.

See Sally During WWII

Because of Daddy's age and the fact he had served in France during WWI, he was exempt from service in the second World War. However, he served as a Civil Defense Air Raid Warden for our neighborhood. After brief training he took charge, making sure the houses showed no light once an air raid siren blasted the air. The blackouts, meant to protect our country from enemy planes that might have flown over, brought Daddy out to walk the perimeter of his designated section. He took his responsibility seriously as part of the war effort.

San and I spent much of our time in school and outdoor play, but WWII always hovered in the background of our minds. Mom helped us write letters to our cousin Herb, a sailor stationed in the Pacific. As we placed a three-cent stamp on each letter we sent, we felt so proud when he wrote back to us. Most of our cousins were closer to Jo's age than ours, and we idolized them. Herb looked so handsome in his navy blues that we couldn't help but fall in love with him.

Every week the rag man came down our alley shouting, "Rags, rags." He drove a wagon pulled by a dappled horse, collecting old rags to be recycled for the war effort.

Mom felt the sting of rationing as she substituted other sweeteners or used less sugar than recipes called for. Everyone made sacrifices for the welfare of our men fighting in Europe and Asia. Using small red coupons, housewives purchased a limited amount of butter, fat and oils, meat, dried beans, canned fruit and vegetables, some clothing, and shoes. Rationing also included tires, gasoline, and fuel oil, the amounts dependent on family size. Drivers were urged not to exceed 35 miles per hour to obtain the most use from each gallon of gas.

Many of our neighborhood houses displayed blue stars in their front windows, designating that they had family members serving our country. A gold star meant someone in the household had sacrificed his life in the war.

We often walked with friends to the Minnehaha Avenue theater for Saturday matinees, and before the main feature we got to watch a short film about the war. The newsreel kept us up-to-date on where battles took place and other pertinent information about the war effort. Matinees cost ten cents.

When San and I joined the Brownie Scouts, with Mom as our leader, she made sure we had a chance to contribute toward winning the war, just like Daddy did. She took our little troop downtown on the streetcar to the Red Cross headquarters where we rolled strips of cloth for bandages and helped collate instructional pages for people involved in the war effort. And being a nature lover, she took us on treks to learn about the flora and fauna in Minnehaha Park. With Mom's help, we earned numerous badges to sew onto our Brownie uniforms.

See Sally Laugh

Because San and I loved to read, we never became bored. In fact, many days throughout our entire young and teen years, Mom yelled at us.

"Get your nose out of that book! You have dishes to wash." Or food to cook. Or cleaning to do. At night we often "borrowed" Daddy's flashlight and read under the covers. Nothing stopped us from reading. Except play.

With friends we played jacks on our sidewalk. We jumped rope. We played hopscotch. Turned cartwheels on our front lawn. And by our garage we played Annie-I-Over. Many summer nights saw us playing until after dark.

Around the age of nine, we received the Christmas presents of our dreams. Bicycles! Although used, they gave us more freedom than we could imagine. San's blue bike came from Jo's best friend Nancy, who, like Jo, was a high school senior. Mine, a red boy's bike, had been our cousin Myles's. He, too, had reached past the age of bicycle riding. I had trouble getting used to the bike's horizontal bar but, with much practice, managed to throw my leg over it with ease.

Sometimes San rode on the bar while I pedaled. I hardly saw past her head, which caused us one day to drive smack into a parked car. Over we went. Bruised but intent on reaching our goal—Minnehaha Park—we kept going.

With our newly-found freedom, Mom stretched our boundaries to include several blocks in each direction. We took off with our friends for the "Giggly Hills," a series of downhill slopes leading to the Mississippi River caves. The adventure later sparked a poem in my mind.

Sunday summer skies clear and blue as a brook
Beckon us to Mississippi's hills
We mount our bikes, mine a boy's style—
heavy, cumbersome as a cement boat
Joining friends, my twin and I pedal hard down River Road
Across lawns, through alleys, onto hillside meadow
Stop, relish the scene below
Steep hills sheathed in green
Wind tickling earth's belly in shimmering waves

Three domes rising and falling to touch water's edge
Three hills to conquer, down up down up down
My heart races I clutch tight to my life raft on wheels
Bike sails down then up then down
Stomach lurching I swallow a giggle
It escapes like bubbles in whitewater's aftermath
Down up down. Hands white, I force a skid, stop at water's edge
We laugh like happy clams in gravel bar
Somber now, restless current matches our hearts
We leave, reluctant, with promise to return
Upstream we edge our bikes up the first mound
Race down to catch a go up the next, the last
Winded, we collapse on river of grass, giggle, roll
Vow to return tomorrow

With each trip, we explored a cave or two, afraid to enter too far for fear of the dark and unknown. To our amazement, we always returned home safe and sound.

We also rode to the Minnehaha Falls public library where we loaded up with new books. Every summer the library staff held a contest. Each young reader kept track of how many books they read over the summer, and the winners won a prize. I don't remember ever winning, but I do know that one summer I read over 100 books.

Minnehaha Park became a favorite playground for us and our friends. One day in late summer we decided to walk behind the famous falls. Our girlfriends joined us in the dangerous exploit. They pushed me ahead to lead the way along the narrow, slippery ledge. San followed me, clutching my dress, while our friends brought up the rear.

I kept thinking. *Don't look down at the spray. Take it slow. Don't slip on the slick path. Don't fall on the rocks below. Don't let San push me. Don't tell me to hurry, San. I can't.*

The watery tumult was an arms-breadth away, the narrow path becoming narrower and narrower. My bare toes curled to hug the muck on the curved, slanted path. I grabbed at the slippery, gray wall but it had no handhold. The steady roar of the falls made me want to scream. Or did I? There was no returning. Finally I passed the narrowest spot and my steps grew longer.

Wet with spray, I pushed my legs for a final, triumphant jump beyond the falls. This was one race I vowed never to try again.

Another adventure we took proved not so dangerous, but memorably humorous. One early summer evening, Mom told us she and Daddy were going for a ride. "Be sure to stay in the yard, kids," she said.

Two of our girlfriends showed up. We turned somersaults and practiced doing cartwheels, waiting for darkness when the fireflies would appear. Then we heard a fire truck go by a few blocks away.

"Let's follow the truck," our friend Carol said.

"Yeah!" San answered.

"But we're not supposed to leave the yard." I scowled at her.

"Oh, come on, Sal. We'll just be gone a few minutes."

"But I have to go to the bathroom And we're barefooted," I whined.

She pulled me toward our bicycles. "I told you not to eat so much watermelon, didn't I? Come on, hurry. Carol and Donna are already on their way."

I couldn't be left behind. Maybe I could hold it until we get back. We pedaled hard toward Hiawatha Avenue, a busy thoroughfare which Mom had warned us not to cross. My mind wavered between my bare feet hurting from the hard bike pedals and my bladder which seemed to swell by the second. Maybe we could stop at a filling station on our way home.

When we reached Hiawatha, we had to stop for the red light. I crossed my legs while we waited for the light to turn green. When it did, San ran her bike across the busy street. I followed behind her, next to Carol. Halfway across the four lanes of traffic, I stubbed my toe on a stone and my bike swerved toward hers. The front wheels collided, jamming the spokes into a lock tighter than a bear hug.

Carol looked at me and giggled. That's all it took. I felt my own giggle rise up in my brain, work its way out my mouth and down my body—down, down, down, stopping in my nether regions. I wiggled and waggled. I doubled over. I scrunched down on my haunches. But nothing stopped my hysterical giggles and, inevitably, a warm liquid ran down my legs, around the soles of my feet, growing into a puddle beneath me. The puddle broke free into a stream headed for the gutter at the curb.

The lights turned red. Cars honked. Drivers shouted. San waved frantically from the safety of the sidewalk, which seemed a mile away. Carol and I finally limped our locked bikes across, where we met her and Donna. Fire siren forgotten, we managed to free our bike wheels and start for home. Carol and Donna left for their houses and San and I rode the final block home, arriving in our front yard just as our folks pulled in by the garage at the alley. We threw our bikes to the ground before meeting them in the back yard, both of us trying to look calm.

"Were you okay here alone?" Mom looked anxious.

San giggled. "Sal wet her pants."

"What? Right at home? For shame!"

I felt my face flush. "Guess I ate too much watermelon," I whispered, before rushing inside to the bathroom.

And speaking of water, Daddy took us fishing one day. He loved to fish and thought we'd enjoy fishing for bullheads near Minnehaha Falls. Minnehaha Creek flowed year-round, so it always hosted fish of one species or another. We caught one large bullhead that day. Once home, Daddy beheaded and gutted it, then nailed it by its tail to our backyard elm where he skinned it in one motion from top to bottom. Mom fried it into a tasty dish that night.

Listen, Sally, Listen

Twice a year our fifth- and sixth-grade classes attended a special event at the large Minneapolis auditorium. I could hardly contain my excitement as we boarded a yellow school bus and headed downtown. How the bus driver must have cringed at the racket we made. My head bounced with the noise of sixty other excited kids.

One time, we were treated to the majestic play, *Heidi,* which later became my favorite book. Another time we enjoyed the play, *Rip Van Winkle.* For days I thought about the man who slept for twenty years and missed the American Revolution, wondering how I'd have felt after such a long nap during crucial times.

Yet another trip took us to hear a youth concert by the Minneapolis Symphony Orchestra. Again, excitement gripped me—not only to be released from the drudgery of the classroom for an afternoon, but to hear a new type of music.

Neither Mom nor Daddy listened to music on the old Motorola radio at home. Daddy had been quite a dashing blade as a young man, enjoying the dance parlors.

Over time, he exchanged that pastime for the gambling booths in local bars. Naturally, that created tension between Mom and him. The only music we heard came from their strident voices.

San and I had never heard classical music. We didn't know what it was. But we could hardly wait to hear it. Once we stepped off the bus and joined the endless crowd of fifth and sixth graders from other buses throughout the city, we stuck together like the well-chewed gum we left nightly on the backboard of our bed. We held hands, afraid we might get separated in the vast, dimly-lit auditorium.

Long rows of cushioned seats filled quickly. The floor slanted, allowing kids in the far back to see as much as those in the front. Our class filled a section in the center. We pulled our seats down, reveling in their velvety softness.

The clamor of thousands of kids didn't stop until the last bus had unloaded and everyone had found a seat. Then, instant silence as the lights went out. A long, heavy velvet curtain parted, revealing the orchestra already seated. When the baton-wielding maestro walked onto the stage, the orchestra members arose in one silent motion. All we heard was the swish of long, black skirts worn by the women musicians.

When the maestro bowed to the audience, I felt my skin tingle. He turned, signaled the orchestra to sit and raised his baton. Members in one breath positioned themselves to play.

The beauty of Tchaikovsky's *1812 Overture* and part of *The Grand Canyon Suite* by Grofe melted my heart. My eyes welled with tears at the emotion of such a sound. For ninety minutes I was transported to heaven with the angels, who graciously bestowed me with a new, lasting love for classical music.

See Sally Tempted

About the time the war ended, our biking escapades took us down neighborhood alleys where we sometimes stole our neighbors' apples that beckoned us as they hung over the fences. But stealing apples didn't seem like real thievery. One time, San and I rode with a couple girlfriends to the Ben Franklin store on Hiawatha Avenue. Our goal was to steal a tube of lipstick. Kyping apples was one thing. After all, the owners wouldn't miss an apple or two. But stealing from a store? After eating a stolen, green apple, my stomach always seized up. That was nothing compared to how it tightened just thinking about the illegal and immoral deed of stealing from a store.

The few hours we'd spent in a Baptist Sunday school class paid off the day we followed behind our friends on our used bikes. Those few hours almost didn't pay off.

By the time we had crossed Minnehaha Avenue and parked our bikes outside the store, sweat slicked my hands and ran in rivulets down my back.

San and I walked in, shy and scared, bringing up the rear as usual. My heart jackhammered, as I viewed the bins of colorful lipsticks, rouges, and powders. I sneaked a quick look to the right and to the left at the clerks busy at the front till.

Quick as the squirrel that snatched a peanut from my mom's hand earlier that day, I grabbed a tube of lipstick. If only I had worn my dress with pockets, I thought. I drew my fist around the tube, walking away as nonchalantly as possible. It felt as big as a softball in my sweaty palm.

I didn't dare look at San. Did she steal something, too? At that moment, however, I didn't feel the symbiotic closeness to her that I usually did. A thief was on her own, I realized. Questions bombarded my quaking mind. Would I go to jail if someone caught me? What would Mom say? Why would I need lipstick, anyway? I was only ten. Would our friends keep their stolen items?

What would God say? As little tykes, we had attended Baptist Sunday school classes with our neighbor, Mrs. Walman. Did one of the Sunday school lessons I had learned enter my mind then? Something subconscious stopped me from leaving the store. As furtive as before, I walked back to the lipstick bin and, again checking to my right and left, dropped the tube into the bin.

Without waiting for San or our friends, I dashed outside where San waited—empty-handed. We smiled at each other before mounting our bikes for the trip home.

Learn, Sally, Learn About God

All moms wore dresses back then. Because money was in short supply in our household, *our* mom made most of hers out of cotton calico. She always wore an apron, too. Because she had no "fancy" or "go-to-church" dresses, we didn't go to church. But I owe my beginning faith to her example of godliness in the home.

My sixth-grade principal allowed us to attend Released Time Education (RTE) each Wednesday afternoon at a neighborhood church. Students could choose not to attend, but most did. Some went to the nearby Roman Catholic Church, some to the Baptist, and the rest to a little Lutheran church about four blocks away.

Daddy's religious inheritance came out of the Norwegian Lutheran Church back in the old country where two of his older sisters had grown up. Daddy had no desire to keep up his family tradition and spent most Sunday mornings sleeping off his Saturday night revelry from hours spent with his buddies at a local bar.

Mom, however, grew up in the church. When her parents settled on the

North Dakota prairie in 1905, the year of her birth, they donated an acre of their homestead for a church and school building. Grandma started and led the Sunday school there and played the piano each Sunday morning during worship. The newly-formed group acquired the services of a Congregational minister, since he also pastored other neighboring congregations.

Because there were no Congregational churches in our Minneapolis neighborhood, Mom chose the Lutheran church as the one we should attend for our RTE. Mom hadn't approved of our earlier lessons at the Baptist church, apparently believing the Baptist influence too strong for our "formative minds." She had stopped us from attending that church.

But Mom never knew how those Sunday school lessons affected my spirit. As a quick learner, I memorized Bible verses and received more than one attendance pin before Mom pulled us out. After that, we spent most Sunday mornings reading the comics of our Sunday newspaper.

With that tiny spark of spiritual understanding, I looked forward to Released Time hour during sixth grade. Like most of my friends, I reveled in the break from studies. We marched from Hiawatha School to church two by two with our girlfriends down the sidewalks, giggling and jostling each other whenever a boy tried to get close. In the winter we ended up in snowbanks, arriving with wet feet and hands because our two-by-two march became undone. Throughout those trips, San and I always made sure we stayed close together.

One week, on arriving at the church we stopped giggling, our hushed whispers more in keeping with the ambiance of the beautiful sanctuary. After shedding our wool jackets and wet mittens in the foyer, we entered the sanctuary for a time of singing and prayer. I paid little attention to the songs, more intent on drinking in the beauty of the stained glass windows.

From there we divided into small rooms for Bible lessons. Each time my turn came to read or share a thought, my face flushed with embarrassment. As my heart pounded, I whispered my answers. In spite of my shyness, however, I retained many of the teachings. I learned the Lord's Prayer. I memorized the Ten Commandments and short Bible verses, though I had no Bible of my own.

Part of our class time included working on simple crafts, singing songs, and practicing for the Christmas program. Because of our shyness, San and I refused to participate in the program, but remembered hearing the Christmas story at the Baptist Sunday school. My heart and soul had absorbed, like a dry sponge, the beautiful story about Mary and baby Jesus.

During the Christmas program, every spiritual feeling flew out of the stained glass windows when two boys from our class wiggled their way on each side of me, separating me from San. The crowded pews meant I had to *touch* those boys. And without eye contact with San or my girlfriends, I felt as stifled as if I'd been caged. I clenched my arms close to my body, keeping my eyes focused on my folded hands until the long program ended. Tears of mortification dripped from my eyes.

The boys must have realized how their teasing brought me to tears, because on the way back to school they acted like perfect gentlemen, much more subdued, to my relief.

Such a fragile beginning to my spiritual education. The soil of my heart may have been dry and unfertilized, but the lessons I learned during those Released Time classes took root during my teen years. Mom may not have gone to church, but she practiced her quiet Christian faith every day. She continued to water my own budding faith throughout all my school years. By her example of integrity and love, she gave me a heart for God.

See Sally Say "Z-Y-X"

Our favorite place to visit during our adolescent years was the little town of Range, Wisconsin, where Grandpa and Grandma Bunker lived, about 70 miles northeast of Minneapolis. We itched with excitement for the time we'd spend in the fresh, country air with Grandpa and Grandma. But again, we had to endure the scratchy horsehair seats in Daddy's old, black Chevy. We wore shorts on the hottest days, but slacks didn't prevent us from itching, either.

During one visit, the air already moist and heavy with heat when we left home, the car gasped as it inched up one hill after another. Along a sizzling, concrete highway then onto blacktop we traveled, and finally down a narrow gravel road to their farm.

We ignored the sweat rolling down our foreheads. At age eleven and a half, it didn't matter. Our parents looked miserable, their own sweat forming dark stains on their clothing. They shifted forward in their seats, the fabric of their clothes smacking like bubble gum as it popped away from the rough seat back.

To pass time we recited the alphabet backwards, racing to see who would win. The only time we did that was when we thought about Grandpa. He had taught us how to do that when we were barely six. Too shy to recite it to our friends and schoolmates and not want to appear boastful, we repeated it only to each other, to our parents, or to Grandpa. With them, we could feel proud of our accomplishment. And proud of Grandpa for teaching us.

I won the race to see who could repeat the alphabet backwards fastest, so we switched to road games. We counted red cars, blue cars, black cars. We recited road signs and advertisements. We read more Burma Shave signs.

When Daddy's car finally coughed its way up the sloped driveway to Grandpa's farmhouse, an old log house built by pioneers years before, Mom's folks greeted us. They didn't kiss and hug and that suited us fine. We didn't do that with Mom and Daddy, why should we with anyone else?

Before lunch (dinner to them), San and I roamed the yard and surrounding area. We reacquainted ourselves with the tool shed and now-empty barn, but stayed away from the occupied chicken house. We pretended we were the original pioneers. We reached up for an old, three-legged stool still hanging from a nail on the rough wall and pretended using it as we took turns "milking Bessie." We scattered imaginary feed to the chickens, keeping our distance. We wished Grandpa still kept animals like he had at their old farm.

We talked about the dairy farm Daddy planned to buy as soon as he took an early retirement from his city job. Then we'd have our own animals and space to play.

We ran through the high grass and weeds behind the outhouse and then along the road. We reveled in the quietness. Wildflowers wafted their sweet fragrance our way. The air seemed purer, more breathable there than in the city. We inhaled the scent of sweet clover from a newly cut hayfield. We skipped down the dusty gravel road, scampering down the ditches to pluck black-eyed Susans and tiger lilies and bee balm. We darted after translucent dragonflies, pretending they'd zip our mouths shut if we dared open them. We listened to chirping grasshoppers and the constant hum of a cicada.

Tall weeds crowded close to both edges of the narrow road. On one side of the road, beyond a wide edge of weeds stood a thick forest of poplars, pines, and maples. On the opposite side lay a hay field. We could barely see the swaths of cut hay over the roadside weeds.

We stopped, frightened, when we discovered we'd gone so far away from Grandpa's, in such a jungle of tall grass and weeds and spooky quietness. We looked at each other and then bounded back to the farm, proving once more we were scaredy cats. But out there no one was around to tease us.

Back at the driveway, we slowed to a walk and caught our breath. We reached the house, ran to the back porch and, once inside, took turns pumping the handle of Grandma's water pump, gulping the cold, refreshing liquid until it ran down our chins and calico dresses.

Mom peered out the kitchen door. "Where have you kids been?"

"Down the road," we replied in unison.

"What did you do?"

"Nothing."

"Don't slam the screen door when you come in," she added. We slammed the screen door.

We devoured Grandma's noon meal of home-grown chicken fried in a cast iron skillet, home-baked rolls, garden-fresh potatoes and peas, and apple pie. We jiggled our legs around the straight-back chairs, eager to get back outside.

"Have fun, girls," Grandpa yelled with a chuckle.

"Don't slam the screen door, kids," Mom said. We slammed the screen door.

We ran barefoot now to Grandma's garden. The sun shone white hot on our dark blond heads. We tiptoed along the warm, soft soil between each crowded vegetable row. We touched the velvet petals of a few pansies as we passed, and plucked a handful of late planted peas. We popped warm, sun-kissed Earliana tomatoes into our mouths.

Mom's garden in the city seemed almost doll-sized compared to Grandma's. Ours separated our back sidewalk and the neighbor's fence on our tiny, city lot. Grandma's garden sprawled in all directions—down the slope toward the side road, up to the woodpile, out into the meadow. Every vegetable we knew of grew there, separated by short rows of brilliant flowers.

When we tired of the garden, we walked to Grandpa's pile of logs for his wood stove. It housed an exciting variety of wild creatures. We crouched close to the outer logs and peered inside between them. Bugs and beetles, worms and centipedes hid under the dried logs. Creatures scampered away when we lifted the rotted bark. Chipmunks scurried up and down, chattering and scolding, running just close enough to tease us. Pine snakes lived under the log pile, and we laughed to see one slither along a rough log. A faint scent of skunk caught our nostrils.

When the sun grew too hot for us, San and I raced back to the house for a drink.

"Where have you kids been?" Mom asked.

"To the garden," we replied in unison.

"Find anything interesting?" Mom and Grandma enjoyed nature, too.

"No."

"Don't slam the screen door," Mom warned.

Away we went again, slamming the screen door.

We raced to the swing, an old car tire tied to a thick rope that was a bit frayed and that hung from a sturdy limb of an oak tree near the edge of the driveway. We took turns on it, pushing each other until we collapsed from heat and exertion. Then we sat on it together, our feet pushing us round and round. We lifted our feet and hung on tightly while we unwound, spinning until dizzy and laughing.

Back to the house we raced for another cool drink of water.

"Where have you kids been?" Mom asked.

"Down at the swing," we replied in unison.

"See anything interesting?"

"No."

"*Please* don't slam the screen door when you leave," she added.

We ran outside, slamming the screen door not quite so hard this time, as we shoved each other in play.

It was time to stalk the grass snakes. We may have been scaredy cats about some things, but not about snakes. We ran around the corner of the house to the shady side and lay down on the cool grass. Stretching out on our stomachs, we inched up to the edge of the porch and peered under the bottom logs into the shadows. Our eyes adjusted to the moist darkness and we remained quiet long enough to watch a grass snake slither our way. We held our breaths. Who would nab the snake first?

I won. Holding it by its neck, I let the body wind around my arm until it secreted smelly slime on my hands. I flung it out into the grass. What fun it was to play like tomboys, when back home in the city with our friends we felt we must pretend girlish fear at the sight of a snake.

To the house we raced, eager to climb the rough, wooden stairs to Grandma's attic. Her treasures kept us there for hours. At one end stood her large rug loom with a partially finished rug, waiting for completion by Grandma's deft hands. On the floor sat baskets of large, colorful balls of carpet rags—fabric strips awaiting their turn on the loom. The floor also held cardboard boxes filled with old wool coats and cotton clothing that Grandma would later tear into strips for her baskets.

During another visit Grandma came up to show us how her loom worked. She sat on a little round seat at one end of the loom, pressing a foot pedal rhythmically to make a maze of heavy white warp thread move up and down, back and forth. At each pedal push she shoved a hand shuttle, connected to one strip of cloth, between the separated warp threads. Her nimble fingers flew back and forth while the colorful rug grew in length.

Grandma made several rugs a day and sold them for 35 cents a running yard. An average-sized rug, at 27 inches wide, cost 50 cents. Customers furnished their own cloth strips, all cut, sewed, and rolled into balls.

During this trip, before we knew it Mom yelled up to us to come down for dinner (called supper in the country). After another scrumptious meal we sat down on the living room rug and played jacks while Mom and Grandma cleaned the dishes.

"Come and comb my hair, girls," Grandpa invited.

We raced to his rocking chair. We ran our fingers along its wide, silky smooth armrests. We caressed the soft black leather of its overstuffed back then took turns combing Grandpa's thick, gray hair. Sometimes we had to stop so he could cough. During his worst asthma attacks, Grandma lit the end of a small, brown, cone-shaped item like incense, and placed it on a saucer. Grandpa then leaned over it, inhaling the smoke that rose from the end. Called Asthmador, the non-prescription incense helped him breathe better.

Soon Grandpa's hair shone like silver moonbeams. We kept combing until he asked us to say the alphabet backwards.

"ZYX," San started.

"WV," I added.

We recited the rest together. "UTS – RQP – ONM – LKJ – IHG – FED – CBA!"

Grandpa laughed along with us. "How'd you learn that so fast?"

"Because you taught us, Grandpa." Again, we all laughed.

Soon after, we went to bed. Grandma made a bed upstairs for us, a thick layer of her old quilts. We used old pillows stuffed with feathers of ducks she had raised many years earlier. We fell asleep long before Grandpa lit his kerosene lamp downstairs, but not before hearing the mantle clock chime the hour.

The weekend disappeared, and soon we sat in the back seat of Daddy's Chevy again. On the way home we were more subdued, each thinking our own thoughts of our next trip to Grandma and Grandpa's. And our family's future farm. Neither could come soon enough.

Love, Sally, Love

Hiawatha Grade School became more to us than mere classrooms. We attended Kindergarten through sixth grade there, loving almost every moment. As pre-teens, we giggled when the boys in our class flirted. We girls stood huddled at the corner of the school during recess, laughing against the cold wind, waiting until the same four boys appeared around the corner every day to tease us. Taking strength in numbers, four of us 11-year-old girls teased back. Alone, not one of us would have dared utter a word to any boy, let alone the four heart-throbs who gave us our reason for living. Together we managed to conquer their hearts with our girlish giggles. And conscious of our immature bodies, we could hardly wait until we looked more like junior high girls, in shape and graceful movements.

I chose Jimmy Johnson as my favorite crush. Already age 12, he boasted a young man's physique, muscles bulging through his shirts. He flicked his sandy, longish hair away from his eyes, the gesture causing my stomach to bounce like effervescent bubbles. During recess, like a forest buck flaunting itself before a doe, Jimmy did a handstand as our group of giggling girls watched in awe. At once he became my hero. I daydreamed about him for weeks. How I managed to retain good grades through my time-stealing crush remained a mystery.

That February, our entire class exchanged valentines. San and I chose small, penny cards wrapped in a package of cellophane, from the Ben Franklin store. We spent the evening of February 13 addressing them, taking special care to give our closest friends the prettiest ones. The leftovers, those with the least loving message, we reserved for the boys. Except my card for Jimmy. I found one with lots of hearts and a romantic message.

The next morning at school, we deposited our valentines into a large box decorated with red hearts. I kept a lookout to see what Jimmy would put inside the box. He sauntered up to it, thrust a pile of small envelopes in, then drew a huge, white envelope from inside his wool jacket, turned to look at me, winked, and dropped it in. I could see that it barely fit into the slot on top of the box.

My heart raced. How would I survive the tedious classroom hours until the afternoon party? Was the big envelope meant for me? I dared hope, blushing to think about it.

When the hour arrived, two girls distributed the valentines as our teacher, Mrs. Fortier, pulled out one at a time and read aloud the name written on it. My heart beat faster with every draw. After what seemed like an entire day, Mrs. Fortier drew out the large envelope. She looked at the name, looked up at me, and smiled.

"Sally Christiansen, it says here," she said, handing it to one of her helpers. Every pair of eyes turned my way. I wanted to slip under my desk and disappear. Yet ... I wanted to snatch it from the girl's hands. I tried to tune out the titters coming from our girlfriends—and from San seated next to me. Once in my hands, however, shaking as they were and knowing my face had turned red as a cherry, I dared open it.

Inside was the most beautiful valentine I'd ever seen. The message could have been meant for an adult, with its romantic overtones. Trimmed in white lace, the front page was softly padded. A big red heart said, "To My Valentine." On the inside, below the sweetest verse ever, he had signed in bold cursive, "Love, Jimmy."

Turning it over, I saw the price marked at the bottom. One dollar! I could have fainted. Did he care for me that much? Never had I been treated with such extravagant care, such love. Although my feelings for Jimmy later faded, I saved his card for years.

Besides Valentine's Day parties, Hiawatha School offered other fun activities. A skating rink filled the ballfield, one we took advantage of many early winter evenings. And of course, even at our age, we used the swings and teeter-totter during recess.

Toward the end of the school year, Daddy and Mom started looking for a farm in northern Wisconsin, as Daddy would be retiring. At odd moments we wondered if we'd miss our school and friends. But for the most part, we kept enjoying our outdoor activities around the neighborhood, relishing the freedoms Mom allowed us.

By this time, Jo had graduated from high school and moved into a girl's club downtown, near the place of her first job. She also spent several months in Chicago working, but nothing was ever spoken of her trip. All we knew was that we missed her.

See Sally Scared

Come September, we headed to a new school—with reluctance.

Sanford Junior High scared us with a capital S. After attending a two-story, six-grade school, Sanford seemed like a city. And twice as far to travel from our house than to Hiawatha Grade School. At least we had neighborhood friends to join us on our walk there and back.

But the walk became the least of our worries. We seventh-graders felt overwhelmed by the constant activity of big, brawny, rushing ninth-graders. For the first time ever, San and I had to be separated. Without each other for moral support, we panicked. How would we remember which room held our class? Why so many separate classes? Why so many teachers? And why not more time to go from one class to another? The five minutes allowed should have been ten.

At least we shared the same homeroom—and found it. Our first homeroom experience, however, was steeped in the teacher's do's and don'ts that swam through our brains like squishy garden slugs. We had to face it. We were on our own. Promising to meet at lunchtime, we separated and walked to class, both of us reluctant to take our first steps down different hallways. With one last look back at San, my safety net, I wondered if I saw tears in her eyes. My own threatened to overflow, but I swallowed hard, determined to go on without her.

It took me days to memorize the way to my locker. How would I remember the locker number among the rows of others? And its combination? Which study book would I need next? Could I drop off those I held or should I take them with me to the next class? Nor could I remember which hall to take to which class. Would I be late for class again? How could I ask someone in the hallway where I should go when everyone hurried, even ran, back and forth? Besides, most students were bigger than I was. Where was San when I needed her? I couldn't remember the names of my teachers, either. And I sometimes lost my homework. For years afterward I had nightmares about losing my way.

The required class I remember most brought me to tears. The dreaded Home Economics class, led by a crotchety, gray-haired woman, demanded that we sew an apron. By hand. Made of a stiff, canvas fabric, the apron tied around our waist. Each stitch had to be precise. San, always more careful about details than I, excelled in her class. I did not. Gritting my teeth and mumbling under my breath, I ripped out the stitches more than once. San won that race with ease.

But we both suffered through the first twelve weeks of Sanford Junior Horror School gladly, knowing we would be moving to Wisconsin by Thanksgiving. No more lost lockers and testy teachers. Daddy bought a farm.

See Sally Farm

In November of 1948, a month before our twelfth birthday, Daddy retired from his Minneapolis School Board job and bought a small farm near Frederic, Wisconsin. He made arrangements for Shorty Aubert, a rural Frederic resident who owned a dray company, to haul our furniture and deliver it the day of our move. How excited we were to be finished with Sanford Junior Horror School.

Mom and Daddy hoped to arrive at our new house before cold weather set in, but winter had begun. The seventy-mile trip north in Daddy's poorly-heated car brought shivers to us as we huddled in the back seat. I had the flu so the trip was doubly miserable for me. When we arrived, we shivered even more in our yet unheated new house. In no time, however, Daddy had filled the basement furnace with wood previously delivered, and we stood over the large, square register between the living and dining rooms. Shorty arrived soon after with our furniture, which he and Daddy set in place before nightfall.

It took forever for our two small upstairs bedrooms to heat up. We each had our own room but always slept together for safety's sake. After all, there was no telling when a scary ogre would be lurking in one of the under-the-eaves closets or under our beds.

Mom wasted no time in enrolling us at the Frederic Grade School. While we waited in the principal's office, he paged Catha Taylor from her eighth grade classroom to the office where he introduced us and asked that she help us find our correct school bus after the day's classes. I rode home to sleep off my fever.

Catha lived with her six sisters and brothers a quarter mile south of us. We became good friends and she introduced us to a new world of country fun. In no time, she invited us to go sledding with them, letting us take turns sliding down their steep hill, using their sleds. We joined them after school and on weekends and became big fans of winter sledding. Soon we began to beg for our own sleds. Always a little fearful of Daddy telling us no, we begged Mom, who in turn begged Daddy. Stuck on the farm, he had fewer occasions to hang out at the bar and gamble, but money remained a big issue in their marriage. He wanted to keep complete control of it, withholding even a small allowance for Mom to use for extras.

He finally relented, saying we could have new sleds for Christmas, but he refused to drive us to town—two miles away—to buy them. One cold December Saturday, Mom and San and I walked to town. Mom led us to the local Coast-to-Coast hardware store.

Inside the store, one whole aisle held an astonishing row of gleaming sleds hanging above the shelves. The variety boggled our brains. Some sleds were trimmed in red, others in blue, still others in shiny gold. We saw sleek ones, short ones, and silver ones. We couldn't decide between those with fancy runner blades that curled at the ends or the ones with lightning streaks painted on the top boards. All of them had ornate cross boards that made turning easy. Our decision wasn't.

Finally, after much thought and quiet discussion, San and I decided on identical Silver Streaks. Our feet danced with impatience while Mom paid the clerk. Proud as princesses, we pulled our long, sleek sleds through town—past the brick high school on Birch Street, around the corner and a half mile to Gunlach's, then past the Java place, Hoosier's sugarbush, and Eklof's farm. Impatient with Mom's slower pace, we finally reached the top of Taylor's hill, a half-mile from our farm.

San and I grinned at each other before plopping onto the shiny surfaces of our sleds. Stomachs down, heads up, we pushed off and ... soared. Faster and faster we went, steering with unerring accuracy down the middle of the snow-packed, gravel road. Sparks flew when the steel runners hit an occasional piece of gravel. The Silver Streaks lived up to their name as they propelled us down the steep hill, then up nearly to the top of the next hill by Taylors' upper driveway. We rolled off our new sleds, giggling, to wait for Mom.

Two of the Taylor girls, Catha and Margie, met us at the road.

"I see you got your own sleds," Catha said. "Come on down after dinner and we'll go sliding."

Now that we lived in the country, we joined everyone else in calling our noon meal dinner and the evening meal supper, with afternoon, light lunches to keep us from hunger before supper, which came after chores.

During our previous years in Minneapolis, we had shared a small sled which we used in the neighborhood on flat terrain. We had no idea sledding on hills could be such fun.

We had already determined that the Taylor kids were our favorite new friends. We had been sledding with them many times, grateful for their generosity in sharing their sleds. Now we could hardly wait for Mom to fix our dinner so we could be off again. No more would we have to use the Taylor kids' sleds or go sliding only when it was convenient for them to go. No more would we have to wait our turn, stomping our feet and clapping our hands to keep the cold from seeping through our wool socks and mittens. We had our own sleds now. We could go sliding any time we wanted. Silver Streaks, here we come!

We gave those sleds a workout during the next six winters. Dressed in wool snow pants, wool jackets, wool caps and scarves and mittens, and rubber boots, we always came home soaked and with chilblains (a painful, itching swelling on our feet caused by exposure to cold). We also brought home red noses and cheeks, aching ears, and chapped wrists and ankles. And of course, always a big smile that kept us rich in memories of our identical Silver Streaks.

Read, Sally, Read

The Frederic Grade School offered an ample supply of books in each classroom. It didn't take me long to read through all the ones I wanted. Then what? How could I survive without books? We learned that the Frederic Public Library, a block away from the school, was open every Saturday.

The tiny building, hardly as big as our two small bedrooms, held row upon row of bookshelves from floor to ceiling. Near the door stood a wood stove, and a desk for the librarian. The pungent aroma of wood burning welcomed me on cold winter days as I focused on the young adult books section. I read any books I could find about girls and their horses, nurses, and adventuresome teens. Any book that portrayed a hero who rescued a girl in trouble caught my fancy. I also read stories about animals, geography, and people fighting in the Revolutionary and Civil Wars.

At home I snuck Daddy's adult fiction books to read in bed. *Forever Amber* and others helped me develop a better vocabulary and offered me glimpses into the world of adults who struggled with life problems.

And one of my first problems became that of finding my way around the neighborhood. Until our move, I'd paid little attention to directions, always using landmarks to tell me where I was and where I should go. Country life changed that for me. I began to read maps, learning that our berry patch at the end of our forty was north of the house. That highway 35 lay at a northeast angle and Clam Falls Road went straight east. Geography became my second favorite school subject, eclipsed only by English.

Mom must have noticed both San and me squinting while we read, for she whisked us off to the local optometrist. Sure enough, we needed glasses. When we wore them for the first time, we couldn't get enough of looking at the colors of the leaves on our lilac bush. Everything popped out in vivid hues. After that, we took them off only for bathing and sleeping. And if by accident we grabbed the wrong pair, the mistake became evident immediately, since our eye prescriptions differed. Not by much, but by enough to notice.

Run, Sally, Run Scared

As much fun San and I had in our new Wisconsin home, we dragged our fears of the dark and birds with us from Minneapolis. In fact, we developed some new fears. Our biggest fear soon became the basement. Back in Minneapolis, we rarely went down into the basement. Here on the farm, Mom found many reasons for us to descend the open stairs into what I thought of as a dungeon.

"Sally, go bring up a quart of blueberry sauce," she'd tell me.

But I rarely went alone. Nor did San. With every step we took down those nine basement steps, I envisioned a creature, a bogey-man grabbing my ankle from beneath and between, pulling me down to devour or torment. The only illumination in that dungeon, a 40-watt ceiling bulb next to the cavernous furnace, cast little light. Around its reach all was shadowed—the corner where Daddy kept an old broom and shovel in a closet just big enough to hide someone; the outside south wall with its small window above, held shut by a flimsy eye-hook; the unusable, darkest corner end of our "pantry."

Along the east side, a hole had been chiseled into the thick, cement wall, large enough for a person to climb through. The hole accessed a large crawl space under our enclosed back porch. Winter and summer, the basement smelled musty because of the dirt floor inside that hole. Water pipes ran under the porch floor, hence the open hole to allow heat from the basement into that area during the winter. Sometimes it grew so cold outside that Daddy placed a heat lamp by the pipes to keep them from freezing. He didn't like the job of checking the heater in the middle of the night for possible fire danger.

Immediately in front of the bottom step loomed Mom's long, wide canning shelf—our winter pantry of sorts. It offered the only color in the entire basement, a rainbow of neatly-lined quart jars filled with fruit and vegetables she canned each year. In spite of our fear of the dark basement, we marveled at Mom's rows and rows of peaches, plums, applesauce, blueberries, blackberries, strawberries, green beans, Swiss chard, peas, pumpkin, pickles, pork, beef, and endless paraffin-topped jars of jams and jellies.

The stairs hugged the north wall. Halfway down, another small window overlooked the driveway. The yard sloped toward the basement so the deep window well often filled with rain that seeped in, sometimes flooding the steps and floor. The dampness added to the musty stench.

Overhead, long strings of spider webs stretched from every crack, cranny, and corner of the low ceiling. The place gave us the willies and we always hurried back upstairs after our errands. We kept a dog or two, but farm dogs stayed outside so we couldn't depend on them to walk us down and up those scary steps. Nor could we take our pets to bed with us, where other fears reared their heinous heads. How we would have loved to keep Queenie, our beloved collie, with us. She'd have been our hero, sniffing out the ogres under our bed and in the attic closets.

Second in scariness to the basement was those attic closets. One ran the length of San's small bedroom. Tucked under the north eaves and boasting a three-foot-high door, the crawl space held boxes of extra clothing and Mom's ancestral records that she planned to use for a book she wanted to write about her childhood on the prairie. But she had to wait until she had more time. Though I had my own bedroom, we always slept in that room, taking turns thumbing the light switch off when we finished reading. No telling if a bogeyman had escaped the closet to hide under our double bed, so the unlucky one to turn off the light stretched arms wide, pushed the switch off, and made a flying leap onto the bed. Remembering the movie we had seen with Jo about the hapless victim seeing a skeleton under *her* bed, we never checked under ours. Instead, we leaped and then covered every speck of our bodies for protection.

The other crawl space ran the entire south length of the house. Its tiny door took up space in the other bedroom. Mom stored our Christmas decorations and other household extras in that closet. We kept the room closed. To add to our fear, we often heard scratching noises in the walls. No doubt mice brought those on, but we envisioned ogres deliberately scaring us.

Winter mornings were always cold, as the only heat came from the stairway and a small, one-foot-square register on the floor. And with only two small windows, the room heated up fast in the summer.

The barn held its own things to fear. As much as we loved the farm, we feared getting too close to the cows. Our small barn housed Bessie and Tessie, the huge black and white Holsteins, and Reddy and one other Guernsey. More to our liking were the calves we fed, housed across the cement walkway from the cows. And when it came time to push down the loose hay from the haymow, Daddy took pity on us. He took over what should have been our job—an easy job. But in the high reaches of the haymow flew starlings, the dreaded birds that threatened to swoop down on us.

When the starlings became a nuisance during one long winter by leaving their multitudinous droppings scattered on the loose hay, Daddy decided to do away with them. He took a rifle, borrowed from a neighbor, to the haymow one night after chores. San and I waited down by the cows while Mom sat at the top of the ladder. She shined a flashlight toward the rafters so Daddy could pick them off, one by one. Trouble is, once the starlings saw the shining light, they flew toward it—down, down, down into the barn where we waited. Never did a pair of identical twins move so fast! Screaming, we left the barn for the house where lesser evils lurked.

Summer brought its own fear. During the spring mating season and even beyond, barn swallows by the dozens perched on the electric wire strung from the house to the barn. They let nothing deter themselves from catching bugs and mosquitoes. When we got in the way, they swooped down, nearly bombarding us as we ran. It seemed birds of many kinds held conventions to see which ones could scare us the most.

See Sally Rubberneck

The telephone wires were a different story. We acquired the habit of calling our friends every night. Back in Minneapolis, we merely had to go outside to find friends for fun activities. At the farm all of our close friends, like us, lived in the country. If we had a homework question, a fun event to plan, or a new bit of gossip about a boy, we phoned.

Our heavy, wooden phone was mounted on the kitchen wall, not too far from the basement stairway. The receiver was attached to the phone by a long wire. Our conversations could not be private from Mom and Daddy, so we kept our voices low when speaking to our friends.

Our party line ring was one long and four short. To reach our friends who had their own party lines, we cranked the phone handle once and the downtown Frederic telephone company operator answered.

"Number, please," she said.

We answered with our friend's number, she rang it, and we were connected. Easy as pie. We and our friends had much to discuss via telephone. What we planned to

117

wear to school the next day. How to answer number five on our math paper. How we hoped to sit next to our latest heart throb at Friday night's football game.

Sometimes one of our party liners might have an urgent need to call someone. Then we had to ring off. And then, when we heard them ring the operator, we'd pick up our receiver and listen in. After all, we needed to know what caused their urgency.

The whole concept of listening in intrigued us. Too much. Our one neighbor, Shorty Aubert, happened to be onto our bad habit.

"Quit rubbernecking, Twins," he yelled more than once, his strident voice blasting our ears. Embarrassed, we replaced the receiver as quietly as a cat after a mouse.

Whether calling or listening in, the black crank phone became our best friend during our teen years.

See Sally Work and Play

Somehow we survived most of our fears by the time summer arrived with its long, sunlit days. As in Minneapolis, we spent as much time outdoors as possible. Unlike in Minneapolis, our outdoors fun usually involved work. Pulling garden weeds. Picking wild raspberries, blackberries, and chokecherries. Shocking grain. Pulling wild mustard weeds in the fields. Picking rocks. Peeling potatoes and making desserts for the regiment of neighborhood grain thrashers who stayed for noon dinner and afternoon lunch when it came to be our turn to thrash oats.

Our very first paying job to earn money for school clothes entailed picking pickles. Our girlfriend, Shirley Graf, lived on a neighboring farm where her dad, Johnny, raised cucumbers—called pickles by all the locals. He hired us to pick them when they reached maturity, then hauled them to the local Gedney's pickle processing plant in Frederic. The more we picked, the more money we earned. But picking pickles was not easy. The spines that covered them and their vines pricked our fingers into a

119

mangled mess. The sun beat down with relentless regularity, causing terrible thirst.

We hadn't picked for more than a few days when San and I both were attacked by the stomach flu. I made it into Shirley's house in time to vomit my just-eaten sack lunch all over their kitchen floor. San managed to talk herself out of throwing up, but we both soon exchanged our hot spot outdoors for our upstairs bed. We didn't earn much money that first summer. Just enough to buy a new pair of shoes for starting eighth grade in the fall and a couple pairs of work jeans. Mom had to make our school clothes one more year.

Although we didn't earn money picking berries for Mom's sauces and jams, I enjoyed it. A thick stand of wild shrubs and berry bushes grew on both sides of our gravel road, so close to home that we picked whenever we had free time. Across the hay field and pasture at the northeast edge of our farm lay a three-acre piece of thick woods. The neighbor's woods abutted our little thicket, which was just big enough for losing our way as we picked wild berries. We worked with two goals: fill our lard pails and don't get lost in the neighbor's woods.

Mom, of course, made good use of every berry we picked. Her goal each summer was to process 300 quarts of fruit for our supper desserts. Of course, she canned all her garden vegetables, too. No Victory Garden for her now! She planted an enormous garden behind a stand of trees and shrubs, out of view from anyone passing by on the road. By winter her jars filled the basement shelf. As afraid as I was of our spooky basement, I never failed to marvel at the beauty of those colorful jars. They looked like jewels and stood soldier-like in long, precise rows, each bright color beckoning, "Pick me tonight. Your taste buds will love me."

Some of our berry picking work days involved day-long trips to the Danbury barrens with the Taylor family. The sandy soil, as well as the thick undergrowth and scrub oaks that grew up following previous wildfires, produced millions of acres of low-bush blueberries. Picking had to be done on our knees or while stooped over, not an easy task either way. The thick woods allowed little breeze. Sweat dripped from our faces. We didn't dare uncover our arms and necks because of the mosquitoes that swarmed around us as we filled our pails.

In such surroundings, San and I faced the danger of getting lost. We kept our ears open for the voices of our parents and neighbors. But in deep concentration of picking as many berries as we could in a short time, at times no one spoke. So we relied on each other, as usual. And as in any northern Wisconsin forest, we feared meeting a bear. Thankfully, we never did.

In early afternoon we all stopped for a light meal. From our cars came jars and containers kept cool by thick layers of newspaper or towels. We enjoyed the makings for sandwiches, Mom's cold chicken, and lots of Watkins nectar—our choice of orange or berry. The time spent along the sandy road brought rest, relaxation, and an occasional, refreshing breeze.

By the end of the long, hot day, we had amassed a trunkful of boxes brimming with the sweet, purple globes that would end up in jars for the basement shelf.

Not every day meant work. Rainy days and Sundays we spent on our screened front porch. Although facing west, numerous trees shaded the porch. There we read books and talked about our favorite boys. On hot days when our upstairs bedroom grew too stuffy for sleep, we slept on the porch's metal daybed, just wide enough for the two of us.

During our first year in Frederic, two boys who rode the same bus as we did took a liking to us. We liked them, too, and sometimes after school the four of us walked home together. Scared of getting too close, we giggled, shying away from their kisses.

I had few boyfriends, just crushes. Lots of them. In fact, I had a crush on almost every boy in my class over the four years at Frederic High. I had long since forgotten all about Jimmy Johnson, my Minneapolis beau who gave me the beautiful valentine. Next in succession, I chose Jimmy Williams, who walked over to visit one summer day, probably a ten-mile round trip just to see me.

The day he surprised me with his visit I was helping Mom weed the garden About three o'clock, I stood up to stretch my back muscles. I turned my head toward the house and to my unbelieving eyes, Jimmy waved to me from the driveway. Oh, no! I looked down at my soil-blackened knees and my sweaty, sleeveless blouse that clung to me. I drew a grubby hand through my hair, knowing the Toni curls had morphed into kinks.

Desperate, I pulled San's arm. "Do I look like a Kewpie doll? Or worse?"

Mom chuckled and told me to take a break. "Go visit him for a while. I'll make some lemonade. We all need a break."

Off we trudged, Mom in the lead and me in the rear. After she and San went into the house, I sat on one of the steps of the back stoop. Jimmy sat next to me. The steps, barely three feet wide, crowded me close enough to touch his shoulder. I felt my face heat like an iron, and it had nothing to do with the air temperature. Sitting so close to Jimmy made my tongue trip over itself whenever I tried to talk. He must have thought I was the biggest imbecile on the planet.

The bathroom window faced the stoop where we sat. Mom had opened it earlier to let the air in. Every time she or San had to use the bathroom, the noise of flushing embarrassed me to near tears. What did Jimmy think? Neither of us said boo, but I felt like choking. How would I survive this awful, wonderful time with him?

To his credit, he tried to keep a conversation going. We sipped the lemonade

Mom brought to us. She made small talk with Jimmy. I know she liked his nice manners.

I kept stirring the toe of one shoe around a crack in the sidewalk, studying it as if it were the most fascinating book I had ever read. I did love to read, but not cement cracks. Too shy, too embarrassed, I let empty air fill our sparse conversation. My heart beat hard with fear that Jimmy would never want to see me again, but with excitement over his mere presence.

After a long silence, Jimmy stood up, taking my hand until I stood next to him. He looked into my bashful eyes, smiled, and kissed me on the lips before turning to leave. My heart soared for weeks—until I sought my next crush.

Boys and clothes and outdoor chores—such as pushing Daddy's old rotary lawn mower through grass that tickled our toes—took up much of our summer. We also spent time in our spacious yard climbing the gnarled crab apple tree. Or sprawling on a blanket on the lawn with a book in hand.

Our sister Jo, who worked in Minneapolis, treated us to a special shopping spree one summer weekend. That first trip alone—together, of course—took us to the Twin Cities by Greyhound bus. Jo met us at the depot and led us to Dayton's bargain basement to buy school clothes. By that time we had saved a little money from our job picking pickles. How proud we felt, being able to earn our own money and travel alone.

At home we often listened to the old radio that sat on top of our small refrigerator. On evenings while doing dishes, we listened to the Roy Rogers show, Lux Radio Theater, Inner Sanctum, and on Saturdays an opera from the Metropolitan Opera House or a classical concert, live from Carnegie Hall.

And we dreamed about the clothes we planned to sew. We perused the Sears and Wards catalogs for fabrics and skirts and blouses. Ever the organized planner, San kept a list of the clothes we wanted to order for the next fall. We earned our own money for school clothes every summer. San's meticulous list included such new fashions as pedal pushers and soft, angora sweaters. We chose neon orange and green anklets, all the rage. We listed jeans and blouses and underwear. Our favorite items of choice, colorful fabrics from which to sew new skirts, dresses, and blouses, tempted us to make our list too long.

Not all of life consisted of working and dreaming about new school clothes. July Fourth became a special day for us in Frederic. On some Fourths we had to help haul hay, but evenings brought a reprieve. The special Frederic celebration.

One Fourth we attended a talent show with the Taylor kids. People came from many miles and filled every space on the school's football bleachers. Some people had to stand. The Taylors picked us up early enough to get front row seats. My butt got sore from sitting those two hours, but it was worth it.

What a variety of talent! We laughed till our sides ached at the ventriloquist and the two acts that tried to copy the popular radio shows, Fibber McGee and Molly, and Arthur Godfrey. The talent show's host, Cedric Adams of WCCO, quite the cut-up too, came dressed to the nines on his generous form. I began to tire from so many songs by the talent show participants, though. Some of the singers didn't do justice to their song choices. I did admire their courage. I wouldn't have been caught dead singing alone in front of anybody—except San.

We didn't get home until late, after the fireworks over Coon Lake. They didn't compare to the displays we used to watch on Lake Nokomis when we lived in Minneapolis. But as amateurish as it was, I wouldn't have traded the experience for an elaborate big city celebration for anything.

Write, Sally, Write

I couldn't sit and drool over catalog pages forever, like San did. My creative thoughts kept returning to the library books I had devoured. I lived vicariously in those stories. I became the heroine, wearing the style of the day, reacting to each conflict with bravery, and winning whatever battle needed to be won.

Between our seventh and eighth grades, however, I read so many adventure books that I decided to write my own. I believed my story would rival that of *Heidi,* my favorite book.

While doing my chores that summer, I relived the stories of my library book heroines. What great conflict could *my* heroine solve? Where should she solve it? Near my home town? In a hospital? No, she had to live in the mountains. Although I had never seen any, I felt drawn to their beauty, their danger, and their wildness through the descriptions I had read.

Once I decided on the setting, my fingers itched to begin writing. The title, *Wild Hero,* erupted like a Montana mountain stream from my headlong thoughts. But I couldn't bring myself to write it on paper until I developed the roadblocks my heroine had to face in order to achieve her goal, and at what cost.

Her conflicts had to be realistic. I created eight whoppers in my mind, crises that would either make or break my heroine's spirit. The rugged terrain and isolation of her mountain home would become life and death challenges for her. Once my thoughts stirred then settled into a coherent outline, I felt ready to write. But with no writing lessons except those absorbed by osmosis from all my previous reading, could I write my story? Once finished, would it be accepted by my family? By my friends? Perhaps by a publisher?

With trepidation and excitement, I wrote my first words with a heavy-leaded pencil on thick, fuzzy, off-white art paper. My book, *Wild Hero,* began …

"In the foothills of the Rockies near a small town called Dry Gulch, which had 439 inhabitants, stood an old cabin made of logs. Near the cabin was a stream that ran down the mts. The stream was like crystal and people who often visited that country

would make a wish in the crystal clear water. Green grasses grew along-side of the wishing stream and about 5,000 sheep would be grazing on those Montana grasses.

"Betty Jo Kertsen would spend most of her time as a guide to her uncle's sheep because she had nothing else to do. Her parents had died when she was six years old. Ever since then, she lived with her uncle Chris in the lonely, old cabin. Even though the cabin was 43 yrs old, it was very beautiful. The shingles were pale blue, to match the summer skies. Made with the cabin was a small porch where Betty's uncle kept the garden foods and canned berries. Two steps led up to the porch which was also blue-colored.

"It was mid-winter and Betty Jo was putting her dog to bed in the shed. She went to her bed thinking about her dog. Just then, she heard a shrill cry coming from the mountains. She ran to her uncle's bedside where he was almost asleep.

"'Uncle Chris, I just heard King's voice from the mountains!' cried Betty, who by now was hysterical."

As I wrote, my eagerness mounted. I named my chapters, pencil flying. I called the first chapter "The Beginning of a New Life." Seven more followed. "A Birthday Present," "A Search for Nothing," "Outlaw," "At Trial," "Training Prince," "Two Mishaps," and "A New Arrival." Each chapter filled about three pages, back and front, jam-packed with my scribbled words. When I finished writing, I leaned back and smiled.

Wild Hero included everything that could go wrong in the life of a teenage girl living on a sheep ranch. Her dog was hurt. Her uncle became sick. A snowstorm threatened the life of the sheep herd. A ne'er-do-well rancher threatened her livelihood and the life of her uncle, her guardian. A neighbor boy helped Betty Jo get her dog back after someone tried to kill it. Conflict after conflict on page after page to leave the reader breathless. Yet the story followed a theme of victory and survival in the wilds and concluded with hope for the future for characters and dog.

In a race to finish, the process of writing *Wild Hero* took only a few days. I couldn't wait to show Mom. I knew she'd like it. After all, she was a writer, too, and understood good writing. But after reading it, she merely smiled and said, "You must have just read the book, *Heidi.*"

I expected more from Mom. I expected her to praise my work, to tell me I should copy it on her Royal typewriter and send it to a publisher. She didn't even leave any red marks on my story. Perhaps she couldn't squeeze them in between the tightly-scribed words and phrases. Perhaps she believed I'd never be a good writer. Perhaps she laughed inside at my amateur attempt.

I left the kitchen disheartened, but not ready to give up. Soon I had an opportunity to prove my mother wrong.

When school began in the fall, each student had to give an oral report of a book we'd read over the summer. My friend, Shirley Graf, who had many farm chores to do each morning and evening, hadn't had time to read a book. When her turn came around, she was frantic. So of course, I volunteered my book. In fact, she wouldn't even have to read it. I'd tell her the story and she could report on what she heard from my lips.

The day came for her turn. Confident, she gave her report. Confident, I expected a glowing review from our teacher,

Mr. Jarolimek. But the glowing review didn't come. Rather, it was more like a *glowering* review, from Mr. J's countenance. Shirley did not receive an A for her efforts. I was grateful she didn't end our friendship. For Shirley, it meant only a drop in grade. For me, it meant devastation.

Until ... I received my quarterly report card. Stunned, I read Mr. J's remark under the A I received for writing. "Sally has great potential to become a good writer."

His encouraging words never left my mind. I savored them like a piece of chocolate cake.

See Sally Eat ... Again

Why was food so important to me and not to San? Weren't we supposed to be alike in every respect? That's what we'd been told. My food obsession began early, perhaps partly my way of dealing with the stress over our quarreling parents. When I felt anxious, I'd eat. San reacted to stress by not being able to eat. At any rate, eating too often, and often too much, became a lifelong habit. However, because of my metabolism, I remained small until my child-bearing years. But always about 20 pounds heavier than my twin. Darn.

Until the day we left home at age 17, San had to push her way ahead of me for food when she wasn't feeling stressed. She did have to eat, after all, and we did share a sweet tooth. Without fail I reached for the biggest, the most, and the best pieces of any food that caught my eye—or nose. The only thing that saved my sister from losing out entirely happened on the day our mom had had enough of our fighting. She made a new rule. I didn't like it. San smiled at its inception.

"From now on," Mom told us, "when you want to share any food, one of you will divide it and the other will choose." I like to think that was the day San started gaining more weight.

I didn't like weighing more than she did. But that didn't stop me from eating. I'd come home from school and shout, "Food, food! I need food!"

Mom made bread at least twice a week on the farm. She bought a second-hand bread mixer. When the time came to knead the dough, she'd set the big, aluminum mixer on the floor between her legs and turn the crank over and over for ten or fifteen minutes. On days we didn't have school, San and I took turns cranking. I'd linger in the kitchen while the dough was rising and while it baked in the oven. I had the happiest nose in the neighborhood, sniffing her wonderful, yeasty bread.

When Mom pulled the loaves out of the oven and popped them upside down on the big breadboard at its place on the kitchen table, I planted myself next to the loaves until they cooled enough to cut. All the while, I pestered her to cut them sooner. If she left the room, I grabbed the serrated knife and cut myself a thick crust behind her back. I couldn't wait to taste the fresh, fragrant, tantalizing bread. I didn't need butter or jam for that first piece, but savored its yeasty warmth.

Besides Mom's fresh bread, I liked oranges. Each night before bed, I grabbed two and ate even the white pulp inside the skin. I surpassed Daddy's appetite, hardworking farmer that he was, with a breakfast of four bowls heaped with Wheaties and milk. I often ate three double PB&J sandwiches after school.

If eating the most had been a category in a race, I would have won every time.

See Sally Pluck Turkey Feathers

One of the highlights of our summer of 1950 was a three-week visit to Mom and Daddy's relatives near Lanesboro, Minnesota. Uncle Bill and Aunt Fern Christiansen (Daddy's brother and Mom's sister) lived on a state fish hatchery in southeastern Minnesota. Bill worked as a secondary supervisor at the coldwater production hatchery, Minnesota's largest. They visited us on our Wisconsin farm then invited San and me to their place. While there, Aunt Fern would see if she could get us hired at the local turkey plant. Ugh, the thought turned our stomachs but the excitement of a new adventure overturned our hesitancy. Besides, we immediately shared visions of all the school clothes and fabrics we could afford to order from the Wards and Scars catalogs.

Their rural home near a bubbling creek enthralled us. But first things first, in Aunt Fern's mind. She wasted no time in getting us signed up for our first bona fide job, even though we were under age.

Once we were hired, Uncle Bill drove us to town each morning and home after eight hours of what we believed was hard labor. And remember, we feared feathers. The turkey processing plant smelled all the way out to the parking lot, but nothing like it did inside. It reeked. But San, the most determined of us twins, vowed we'd work there anyway. We needed the money not only for school clothes, but also for Greyhound bus travel back home.

Aunt Fern signed us on for three weeks. She had worked at the turkey plant and knew all about it. She assured us it would not be difficult. But determined or not, we couldn't shed our fear. Would a stray turkey fly into the picking room and attack us? Would we be able to keep up with the high, moving assembly line track? We could hardly reach it. And how would we ever manage to pick all the pinfeathers off the dead, blood-dripping birds fast enough?

We had already applied for and received our Social Security cards. We had already met some of the other workers—little old ladies who knew our aunt and worked at the turkey plant full-time. We had already drawn up a lengthy list of catalog items for our prospective purchases. We were ready, fear or not.

Aunt Fern scrounged around for calf-high rubber boots to wear during working hours and gave us scarves to tie around our hair. On day one, the boss patiently showed us how to pick the pinfeathers off each naked bird as it traveled, head down and feet clamped to a hook, on the moving track. "Be sure to get every pinfeather," he warned. "It's easy work, but you must keep up."

The four or five little old ladies working
in the small, dark, smelly room helped us every time the boss left the room. They sandwiched the two of us between themselves so they'd be ever ready to help if needed. It needed!

Our fingers felt like giant thumbs as we struggled to pick the stubborn pinfeathers off the repulsive birds. Whenever we squeezed an extra short pinfeather between our thumb and forefinger, it popped back in—under the turkey skin where we couldn't reach it again. How we struggled to get those darn pinfeathers out.

Noon lunchtime came and we joined the ladies outside to eat a sandwich our aunt had prepared for us. The bad smell made it hard to eat, however. Too soon we had to return to the never-ending line of naked, moving birds. By the time our shift ended, we were exhausted and discouraged. Could we handle another day like this? The boss had looked at us with a frown every time he came into the room. We felt as low as the turkeys with their dead heads hanging down. But between our aunt, uncle, and the little old ladies, we received enough encouragement to pluck on.

Days two and three proved as hard as the first. After that, it became a tad easier.

Every single day of our agreed three-week employment, however, the boss came to us at least once and said, "You'll have to do better." Or, "I don't want to fire you, but ...." Or, "You've got to move faster or I'll have to let you go."

One day during a thunderstorm, the electricity went off. Left in total darkness, San and I nearly panicked. We kept hearing live turkeys in the nearby killing room. But our helpful ladies soothed our fear with kind words and laughter while we waited for the lights to brighten our lives once again.

By God's grace and a few silent prayers, we made it through the three weeks, earning enough money to buy our bus tickets home and most of our school clothes for the coming year. If it hadn't been for those little old ladies helping us finish picking our turkeys, we'd never had made it. Every day they had to work faster to pick their own turkeys so they could help us with ours.

I'd never encountered such kindnesses from strangers. We were grateful beyond words for their help. I didn't remember their names, but kindness doesn't have to remember names. It is given in love by nameless faces and is cherished forever.

Tired as we were by each day's end, and during weekends, we found time to play. Uncle Bill's job offered interesting diversions. We watched him feed the trout hatchlings, walking from pond to pond with a huge, heavy metal bucket filled with red mash. The pond covers looked like glass tents, each closed with a huge, tilted door. As Bill threw the mash in by the scoopfuls, the fingerlings in one pond swam in a frenzy to eat. Then he closed the heavy door and repeated the process at the next pond, which held yearling trout.

Some ponds had no covers. Their fresh water reached almost to the walkway. We clung to each other's hands as we followed Uncle Bill along the narrow, cement path, afraid of falling in. Although we took those walks only when he was with us, both San and I had nightmares about those scary ponds.

I marveled at the sounds of wildlife at the hatchery, which was tucked away in its isolated locale. One night we awoke to a scream. Thinking a woman was in trouble, we made our way down the spiral staircase to tell our aunt and uncle.

"Oh, that's just a bobcat," we were told.

I heard that scream in my mind every night for years.

One part of the hatchery we visited every day was the artesian well which housed a gigantic sturgeon that swam back and forth, back and forth. It helped keep the water clean. A tin cup hung on a post nearby, waiting for us to dip it into the clear, icy cold water for a refreshing drink.

In Uncle Bill's garage-workshop, we helped him crack black walnuts in a vice mounted on one end of a long table. Earlier we had helped him and Aunt Fern pick the nuts from among a nearby grove of trees. Our hands turned black as coal while we husked the soft, thick outer coating from each nut before we could crack them open. Handling the spiny, hard shells brought a different look to our hands, this time a host of tiny pinpricks on our fingers. In spite of the discomfort and efforts involved in routing out each piece of meat from each nut, black walnuts remained my favorite.

Aunt Fern and Uncle Bill saw to it we enjoyed other activities while at Lanesboro. One Sunday they drove us to a motorcycle hill climb at the base of one of the many river bluffs that dotted the country. A rowdy crowd of outdoorsy, sporty folks attended the event, with the roar of dozens of cycles drowning out their din. Along with other spectators, San and I climbed the hill alongside the cyclists, until we heard someone warn about rattlesnakes. We scurried down to our hosts where we stayed for the remainder of the hill climb. Though unafraid of snakes, we knew better than to tempt the bite of a rattler.

One hot, mosquito-infested Friday night, we drove into Lanesboro to enjoy a movie at the outdoor theater. Unlike more elaborate theaters with microphones and parking places wherein one could enjoy the show within the comfortable confines of a vehicle, the one we attended offered long rows of benches in the grass that faced a large screen. Local people visited with one another during the movie as if the occasion were a neighborhood party.

The scariest excursion we took during our three weeks at the fish hatchery involved a neighbor girl, one of Aunt Fern's friend's daughter. Her mom occasionally brought her over to play with us while the two adults visited inside. One day the three of us went down to the nearby creek, crossed its plank bridge, and walked along the banks among thick trees and bushes. We picked our way along the precarious edge, grabbing branches to keep ourselves from falling into the fast-flowing stream.

"Let's cross over," our friend said. Without waiting, she hoisted up her skirt and started across the rushing, rock-infested waterway.

San and I looked at each other, both of us recalling Uncle Bill's warning about staying away from the creek. But … we followed.

Clutching each other's hand as a lifeline, we made our way across. Slowly, slowly we dodged boulders, stepped into unseen holes, struggled to balance against the strong current. Soaked but jubilant, we climbed the muddy, slippery shore and began picking our way back to the bridge where we sat to dry off. No one would be the wiser about our forbidden adventure. Nor would we forget its danger.

Before we left for home on the Greyhound bus, we spent a day inside helping Aunt Fern cut out a dress for her visiting, older aunt. Our great-aunt Eula Beighle, came north every summer from her southern Illinois home to visit relatives. Eula was Grandma Leila Bunker's oldest sibling, who as a young lady had broken her engagement to a young man when their mother died so she could raise her younger brothers and sisters, including Grandma.

While visiting Aunt Fern, Eula wanted us to help her make a couple new dresses. The older, gray-haired woman used a cane and rarely laughed. But we enjoyed helping her. At age 14, we had just started to make our own clothes, so we knew a little about sewing.

The pattern Aunt Eula chose couldn't have been easier. More like a sack than a dress, it fitted her shape well. At her age, style didn't seem to be important. The process of cutting the tiny, flowered fabric brought to mind the more colorful material we'd soon be ordering, once we arrived home.

See Sally Win and Lose

We rode the Greyhound bus home with dreams of new fabric, new clothes for school, and thoughts of sharing our adventures with Mom and our friends. With summer waning, we caught up on our 4-H activities, an organization we joined soon after moving to Frederic. We ordered a host of catalog items and hurried to sew new skirts and dresses. We entered them into the Polk County Fair, winning a few prizes. Mom's help benefited us, though we chafed at the thought of needing help. After all, we'd helped Great-aunt Eula make her dress. Why couldn't we do our own?

San, always the most precise and careful, won more blue ribbons than I did. I hated that she won that race. Why did I always have to be in such a hurry? The constant competition between us often led to fights, allowed our tempers to flair, and kept us trying harder to outdo the other.

We even fought while doing supper dishes.

"I did, too," one of us yelled about a particular oversight.

"Did not."

"Did too." Our words brought on another shin-kicking melee.

During one such scuffle, Mom walked in from the barn.

"Kids! Quit yelling. Do you like fighting like this?"

We looked at each other. Grinning, we answered, "Yes."

Mom sighed. She quit trying to settle our squabbles.

As we grew older, we seemed to take turns winning our races. I read my beloved library books faster but she remembered them longer. She came in second behind me during our grade school spelling bee. I ran a tad faster, grabbed the first slice of Mom's homemade bread, caught the mumps first. She had more friends, had whiter teeth, looked prettier.

But in the eyes of other kids, we were indeed identical. And in spite of our compelling need to compete, as siblings, we stuck together. Shy as two fawns, we rarely parted. Being forced to attend classes separately, like schools later required for twins, likely would have injured our psyche forever. We were that dependent on one another. Rarely did we speak in terms of "I." "We" became the norm of our speech even after we left home following high school graduation.

The world may have seen us as one entity, and we may have been dependent enough on each other to warrant argument from any outsider, but we couldn't stop comparing ourselves with the other. Our 4-H projects had us vying for the most blue ribbons for our county fair sewing and cooking projects. I wanted my skirt to win over San's, my cookies to be touted as the most perfect over hers, my 4-H garden poster display to win the grand prize ribbon.

The first time I gave a demonstration at a county-wide 4-H meeting, I thought I'd faint with fear. I practiced and practiced at home how to make biscuits. I set out every necessary utensil next to all the required ingredients, set in order of use. I measured each ingredient, mixed them by hand, and dropped them onto a baking sheet, all the while explaining to my audience each precise step of the process. To make sure I wouldn't forget a step, I wrote a few crib notes to read because while practicing at home, I always forgot a step or an ingredient. But I managed to succeed in the demo. My crib notes saved the day.

Our independence and competitiveness continued. She had the first boyfriend. I felt envious because she won the title of "Miss Pepsodent Smile" in high school. Our classmates admired her for her neat appearance. Identical as we were, I saw her as more popular, prettier than I. Mom's admonishment about washing my neck cleaner added to my sense of being second best. Yet I kept trying to win a new race between us.

We both wanted to look our best, though I less so, so we curled our hair. Once or twice a year we gave each other a Toni home permanent. The going style of curls made me look like a Kewpie doll. To my eyes, San always looked better. But I hated those perms, probably because my hair had just enough body to make my permed hair look frizzy.

One race I wouldn't touch, was the school's forensic contest. San signed up for it, her decision surprising the gremlins out of me. All along I thought her fear of public speaking rivaled mine, but her best friend persuaded her to enter. I felt jealous, but volunteered to listen and help her memorize her chosen piece. Jealous or not, when she stood before the entire student body and recited, I felt proud enough to choke. It didn't matter to me that while sitting breathless in the front row, I could barely hear her voice. It didn't matter that I saw her knees and hands shake during her speech. All I could think was how proud I felt about her gutsy decision.

San's fierce determination carried her through many problems. I may not have sounded or acted proud of her, but I admired her tenacity since the first day. Being the second born—the "weaker twin," as Mom called her—she had to struggle harder in life for some things. Yet she kept persevering. Like the tortoise who won over the hare, she won her share of our races.

See Sally in High School

High school offered us a variety of extra-curricular activities. At the urgings of our close friends, San and I joined the music class. With visions of playing in an orchestra like the ones we enjoyed listening to on the radio, we chose the trombone. Each week four of us giggly girls sat with Mr. Sommerfeld, the music director, as he *tried* to teach us how to play that instrument. We were all small so the trombones seemed to overwhelm us in size. But we laughed our way through the simple lessons, going so far as to waggle our way onto the school bus toting not only the clumsy trombones so we could practice at home, but armloads of study books. Why Mr. Sommerfeld didn't retire that year after struggling with such silly students is beyond me. We failed in our own eyes but in his as well.

Our attempts lasted a few weeks until all four of us gave up. Then I decided to try the snare drums. I envisioned marching in the school's parades and playing in concerts as I took up a pair of drumsticks. I didn't fail with the drums. In fact, I enjoyed it so much I wished I'd kept at it. But other activities and home chores interfered, causing me to drop out.

Like some students, we often brought our lunches to school. However, we especially enjoyed the school lunches, available at the grade school. In the fall and spring we liked the four-block trip downhill from the high school, but it meant we had to eat fast so we wouldn't be late for our first afternoon class. On days we didn't have to hurry, such as when we were scheduled for Home Room, we stopped at Winberg's small grocery store for a ten-cent ice cream cone. He always filled the cones with two scoops, which we savored while sauntering back up the hill to class.

Most school lunches offered food I enjoyed, probably because I liked most foods. My first taste of lentils came during one of those lunches. I thought it tasted great. Most students disliked it, dumping their meal in the trash can. Too embarrassed to say I liked it, I followed suit but didn't like myself for doing so.

During the early 1950s winters, we experienced snowstorm after snowstorm. On some school days we had to wait at the road for the school bus, as the snowbanks along our driveway reached too high to see the bus coming from our usual waiting spot at the kitchen window. In 1950 alone, blizzards killed 250 people in the U.S. The number is significant in spite of a census population of 150 million.

We loved snow days when we could go sledding with the Taylors. Sometimes Catha's oldest brother hitched a toboggan and all or our sleds behind their tractor so he could pull us along the road. He'd veer from one side of the road to the other, giving us the thrill of trying to stay on without tipping over. Our road had little traffic so in that respect, we felt safe. But when our sleds went faster than the tractor, danger threatened. We could have slid beneath the tractor or into its huge tires. God's angels worked overtime in keeping us safe during our escapades.

4-H activities also kept us busy winter and summer. Besides our leaders helping us prepare for talent shows and all kinds of demonstrations, we enjoyed hayrides and square dances. At one square dance, Mom and Daddy joined us. Daddy took me in his arms and danced with me, the only time he held me since infancy.

Climb, Sally, Climb

One autumn day, Mom overheard San and me discussing the fun we'd had the day before when we and our friends picnicked under the Frederic water tower after school.

"Don't you kids ever climb that water tower," Mom warned.

"Sal already did," San blurted.

I was used to Mom's "don'ts" and this time I turned away to hide my smile of satisfaction. If I'd waited for her permission or waited out all her don'ts, I'd have been unable to try out my teenage wings. The word don't wasn't in my vocabulary when I was young. Too many tantalizing temptations faced me. Not that I was a bad girl, nor did I try dangerous stunts like jumping off a cliff, but I just wanted to have fun and try new things. For me, life presented an endless series of twists and turns. I had to investigate them to satisfy my curiosity. Besides, no one—not Mom nor the law—had told me climbing the water tower was a forbidden activity.

After I climbed the forbidden tower that autumn day, I knew I'd remember forever the scare of the climb and the thrill of the awesome view from the top. It happened like this ...

After we girls had finished eating our packed lunches and had some time to kill before the Friday night football game, one of my friends dared the rest of us to climb the tower with her. San's best friend declined. San tried, but got no farther than the third rung. That left two of us.

My friend led the way. I followed behind her black and white saddle shoes. Since Friday was declared Slacks Day at school, we didn't have to worry about keeping our usual, cumbersome skirts from tangling around our legs.

I clung to the metal ladder rungs, feeling relatively secure by the cage-like frame that enclosed my quivering body. The higher I climbed, however, the less secure the cage felt and the shakier I became. I kept silent, afraid my voice would betray me in wavery ripples. Up, up I went until I finally reached the circular walkway at the base of the high tower. I took a long, shaky breath and walked around the walkway.

Wow! The late September color spread before me, layer upon layer, toward Grantsburg twenty miles away. Golds and yellows and reds and oranges competed with the shadowed, deep greens of pine trees against a blue sky in the late afternoon. The pungent aroma of a bonfire drifted our way from a thin column of smoke off in the distance. Cars whizzed by below us along the highway, their engine sounds muffled. The vehicles looked like racing ants.

Then, San's voice reached us in frantic half-whispers, begging us to come down. I didn't want to leave. I wanted to stand there and savor the beauty forever.

I didn't want to descend the ladder, either. After I had oohed and aahed and pointed out landmarks for a long while, we knew it was time to leave. We had to descend that ladder.

Swallowing hard, I tried not to look down. Such a long way! I tensed my muscles and began the descent, again following my friend. I felt like I had in Physical Ed class when told to climb a rope hand over hand. I had failed miserably. But I couldn't fail now, so my hands gripped the ladder rungs with far greater strength than what I'd had in Phy Ed class. With shaky knees, I found my footholds slowly ... oh, so slowly. When I reached the ground, I nearly fell—from fright or exhaustion I didn't know.

As I looked at my red, stinging hands after collapsing on the picnic bench, I smiled. I had made it through a daunting adventure. More new adventures would face me, some harder than others. But each obstacle, each climb would make me stronger, more resilient, more joyful.

I never did learn if climbing the Frederic water tower was illegal and never tried an illegal activity again ... or did I? If not forbidden by law, my mom had forbidden it, albeit too late. My forbidden activity was worth all the don'ts in her vocabulary. The view alone brought me joy unspeakable.

Hug, Sally, Hug a Tree

Mom knew every tree in our yard. She had tried teaching us about nature as early as when she led us on Minneapolis park treks during our Brownie Scout days. Too occupied with having fun with our friends, we paid little heed. But my interest in the natural world grew.

I especially loved trees. I remembered some Bible verses that talked about trees, giving me pause about the trees that surrounded our farm. One special tree, an old basswood, stood at the top of our hill behind the barn. Its spreading arms opened wide to embrace the sun and moon, the stars and wind, the bugs and beasts—and me. It stood strong and erect, a sentinel that guarded the secrets of our family and farm, secrets buried among the nearby junk and broken cement at the foundation of the farm's original, long-gone house nearby.

The tree's large, heart-shaped leaves fluttered and sang in the wind, beckoning me toward its cool shade. Every summer and autumn I studied it from the back porch or from the upstairs bedroom window, yearning for time away from chores to enjoy its silent, accepting company.

With San as my second half, I couldn't imagine why I'd want to spend time alone at the tree. So we often walked up the hill together. There we watched the squirrels and other small critters scamper around. We inhaled the fragrant wildflowers. We rummaged around the old foundation and, in springtime, hunted for wild asparagus that grew nearby. We kept an eye out for our big cows, knowing we could take hurried shelter in the safety of the tree's lowest branch, if need be.

In my mind, the basswood became a microcosm of nature at its best. But we had to choose our days to visit. Summer storms brought damaging lightning to the hilltop trees. We saw several scars along its trunk. I kept waiting for a windstorm to knock it to its knees. My hugging tree lived for many years. I never tired of visiting it, offering a hug of thanks for its faithfulness and beauty.

See Sally Study

Throughout high school, my favorite classes were English and Home Economics.

I hated Math, passing the subject only through the help of a friend when we studied in the empty sick room. I disliked Science because I couldn't understand it, but gave my teacher silent praise for not failing me. And I disliked Phy Ed because my body balked at being bombarded by commands to be coordinated. Sports didn't interest me, either. When a softball flew my way during a game, I ducked rather than reaching for it. No wonder team leaders chose me last for their team. In a foot race, I always ended last.

English classes kept me interested, if not spellbound, as I learned how to write a well-constructed sentence and why certain famous authors wrote the stories they did. My vocabulary grew through my studies and by process of osmosis as I read book after book. The only part of English I feared was giving oral reports. Through time, I mastered that.

I enjoyed my required Home Ec classes so much that I decided to become a

Home Ec teacher. Until I learned that in college I would have to take a math class. It scared me away.

Not only did I learn how to cook and bake, through hands-on experience, but how to set a proper table and how to plan a food budget. In pairs, we classmates walked to the grocery store, pen and paper in hand, to price and buy food items. The school provided money, through the store's account, for our shopping excursions and, once back in class, we had to account for each item. With eggs costing 24 cents a dozen, ground beef 49 cents a pound, and sugar 84 cents per ten-pound bag, we had to make sure to get our budget's worth.

In one segment of learning about how to keep house proficiently, we had the pleasure—for me, at least—of drawing on graph paper a kitchen and a living room. We cut and glued measured pieces of cardboard onto the graph paper until we had placed all the required pieces of furniture in the most practical way possible.

The class also provided sewing machines. Mom had already taught us how to cut fabric from patterns and how to sew seams, making Home Ec sewing a cinch. San and I competed, as usual, with her winning with the neatest, most precise article of clothing.

One summer we each took on a decorating project, to be graded in the fall, for our bedrooms. Eager to learn how to sew as Mom did, we fashioned window curtains and bedspreads, using Mom's electric Singer sewing machine. The excitement of having our own room—even though we would always sleep together in one of them—grew as we chose the colors and décor.

Because we had learned the folk art of tole painting in Home Ec, I decided to paint my very own three-drawer dresser and matching mirror white, with added colorful scrolls around. I embroidered flowers on feed sack pillowcases, arranged a makeshift bookcase, and hung my meager wardrobe of dresses and skirts and blouses in the miniscule closet. I even sewed a curtain to close off my closet.

Living in the country prevented San and me from participating in many extra-curricular activities that required after-school trips to town. However, we joined the school choir since practices were held during school hours. With weak voices, we didn't contribute too much but enjoyed the efforts. Before acceptance, we had to sing privately in front of the director. Another fear to face. Somehow, we both managed to sing in tune, albeit very softly, and passed muster.

The choir gave two concerts a year, which meant Mom and Daddy had to drive us to school and attend. Mom always came to hear us perform. Did Daddy? Or did he head over to the bar to wait out the concert? I couldn't remember. He did complain often about the price of gasoline, 18 cents a gallon, but managed to take trips to the Lewis bar up the road a few miles northeast.

Our choir competed with other area school choirs, which meant making bus trips to various schools. The frenzied pace of so many students preparing for the competition made me think back on our Sanford Junior High experience. I didn't like it.

Because I enjoyed writing, in my senior year I volunteered to be on the annual class yearbook committee. A group of my classmates worked during their free time to plan and put together the book, but I contributed little. Too shy to share my opinions, I stayed in the background, never having written anything about anyone. Another race lost.

School offered occasional reprieves from study. Each year we enjoyed at least one assembly program. One year a pair of trampoline performers put on a heart-stopping show with their aerial acrobats. The artists asked for a volunteer from the audience. San's current boyfriend gave us a hilarious if not brave show of bouncing on the trampoline. A small, gutsy kid one year older than we were, he probably also was one of the students who rode a donkey during a donkey basketball games at school.

Another program featured a famous yo-yo expert. Luck, Wisconsin, a few miles south of Frederic, boasted of being the Yo-Yo Capital of the World. Dozens of locals worked at the Duncan Yo-Yo toy factory which produced the popular toy for the world market. Of course, after the show, many of us students went out to buy our own yo-yos and practice some of the same moves as used by the experts.

Another interesting but scary assembly program featured a snake handler. San and I enjoyed his talk, since neither of us feared snakes. But those snakes dwarfed the little pine and garter snakes we'd been used to playing with. Again, the host asked for a volunteer. One of our classmates walked up to not only touch one of the huge boa constrictors but to allow it around her neck. She looked nervous but excited. Many of the girls in the audience screamed. We thought she showed bravery.

See Sally Pick

With the diversions of extracurricular fun such as choir and school programs, our studies became more tolerable, just as 4-H and other summer activities helped us more easily accept the farm chores Daddy assigned us.

Every spring before school let out we spent some Saturdays picking rocks. We rode on the hay wagon Daddy pulled behind our John Deere tractor out into the field he had chosen for planting oats. We walked back and forth, searching for rocks that might cause the seed planter or cultivator to break once he began planting. The ground, plowed the year before, was bare of corn stubble so our gaze took in every rock and stone. They dislodged with ease in the soft, loam soil until we found a rock too heavy to lift. Then it took both of us to grab beneath it, struggle to carry it, and drop it into the wagon.

Rock picking meant sore shoulders and sore backs. But farmers—and their daughters—put up with the annoyance every year. I wondered how the rocks seemed to grow as fast as Daddy's crops.

Once the oats and alfalfa matured, we had the dubious pleasure of going through the same fields to pick mustard plants. The yellow-blossomed weed had the reputation of making cows sick. Whatever the reason, the plants had to be picked. We didn't relish that chore, either, especially as it brought us to sneezing by day's end.

Neither the rocks nor the mustard stalks we picked brought us financial reward. However, for two summers we looked forward to picking beans. The chore earned us enough money to buy all our school clothes. But at what price? Unlike rocks and mustard, bean picking required us to get down on our knees or stoop to a much lower level. And it meant working almost every day to keep up with the astounding growth of new beans.

Each year Daddy plowed and disked a five-row section behind the barn and Mom planted the bean seeds. The rows ran downhill to offer good drainage. At least we didn't have to kneel in water. But the year of 1951 was a wet year. Storm after storm came through, thwarting our efforts. The beans back then turned rusty brown when wet, which meant we couldn't start picking until the leaves had dried and wouldn't touch the beans. Rusty beans brought no payment from the Stokely's bean factory in Frederic. Neither did overripe beans, which happened often that summer because of too many rainy days.

Eager to make money, San and I hoed the five long rows, with Mom's help. When the beans grew to proper size, we started picking. It didn't take a day to realize this job wouldn't be easy. As we picked, we often stood up to rub our lower backs before bending over again. When the torture became too much, we dropped to our knees, scooting our way along the rows. Sure did make for muddy jeans, enough to feel the wetness clear to our skin.

"These dumb rows are a mile long, I swear," I complained to San.

She groaned. "Yeah, and I can't stand this heat much longer."

As the chore grew longer, I kept a running conversation in my head. *You can do it, Sal. Only one more row. You can do it.*

Mom joined us in picking on some days, probably bemoaning the time taken away from her own garden and house chores. Every day, it seemed, the worry creases on her forehead grew deeper as she tried to keep up with things.

We toughed out each picking day, except for one thing. Both San and I hated millers, the huge, black moths that hid under the broad bean leaves. They resembled feathers to our fearful minds, so Mom heard plenty of screeching from the bean patch that came when we encountered yet another miller.

After each picking, we dumped our beans from our small galvanized pails into gunny sacks, which Daddy and we took to Stokely's where they were sorted by size. With each paycheck we grew more excited. On the rainy days we scoured the catalogs for the clothes we'd order later.

One rainy day I looked out the kitchen window at the five long rows of wet beans just waiting to dry and be picked. I pictured them as dollar bills that we'd send to Sears, Roebuck for new blouses and slacks and jeans. And for my own choice of fabric to sew into skirts and dresses, unlike those San would sew for herself. We needed only two pairs of jeans a year for working outside in the hay field and helping with barn chores. We needed only one new pair of slacks each, to wear to school on Fridays—slacks days. The rest of our earnings would be for underwear, sweaters and blouses, and my favorite thing, fabric for skirts and dresses.

Mom insisted that San and I keep dressing alike. But as teenagers we put our feet down. No more clothes alike! Besides, we already knew how to sew our own clothes, so Mom couldn't make us buy the same patterns of material.

"Think how much fabric you'll save when you both use the same piece of cloth," she kept arguing.

"It's our money," I pleaded. "Besides, look at the money chart San made. See how much we'll make if we pick a hundred pounds of beans? And if half of them are perfect enough to make Grade One, we'll earn close to three dollars. We figure we can each pick two bushels a day, so that will be at least five dollars every day. Each."

I shoved the list under her nose. "That's a lot of clothes and fabric, Mom."

Her mind was stuck like an old, scratched Victrola record. She looked me in the eye and said, "What if it rains so much you can't pick them every day? You'll have more Grade Three beans than Grade Ones, and there goes your budget."

That was my biggest worry. What if we didn't make enough for everything we'd already chosen from the catalog? How could we pare down our list and choose items we couldn't live without?

The whole summer depended on the bean crop. I thought about what Mom said and formulated my answer. It came to me like a lightning bolt.

"I know!" I told her, turning to grin at San. "We'll pray for good weather. That's what the pastor said we should do. We just studied about prayer in confirmation class."

Mom smiled and walked away, but not before giving us another one of her everlasting warnings. This time, it was "Don't fight while I'm in the garden hoeing. And as soon as you finish the dishes, go out and pull some more weeds in the bean patch."

"In the rain, Mom?" I was incredulous.

"It's not cold out and it's not lightning. So yes, in the rain." She slammed the door behind her.

There went my plan to drool over the Sears catalog again. The fall catalog had come in the mail a week earlier and San and I had spent every minute we could studying the clothes and fabric pages, changing our list every day.

One rainy day San pulled me into the front porch.

"I made a new list of what we should order for school." She pushed her list into my face. "If we sell 120 pounds of beans in the next two weeks, we'll have enough for most of these clothes. And this baby blue felt material for a circular skirt."

"Oh," I sighed. "It's gorgeous! But too expensive."

"We can do it. We *have to* do it."

In the next two weeks it rained many times. Our hopes plummeted.

San chewed the end of her pencil. "If we cut down on other stuff, maybe we can afford the felt material."

Studying her list for the five-hundredth time, we decided to order three blouses each instead of four.

"And maybe scratch our plans for those orange and lime green neon anklets," San said.

"Oh, no!" I yelled. "I'm getting those socks."

Her voice rose over mine. "But then we can't get the blue felt, Sal."

I sighed. She always did get her way when it came to clothes. But I knew her sense of style far exceeded mine. I depended on it. So I gave up my dream of the neon sox. Maybe next year, if they remained in style.

I sighed again, handed her a dishtowel, and ordered, "It's your turn to dry and put the food away. I wash this time."

She kicked me in the shin. "Is not! I'll wash."

Before we knew it, we were fighting again—just like Mom ordered us not to. As usual, I gave in to my baby sister. Baby by forty-five minutes, but she still qualified. She was a tad smaller … and finickier … and weaker. But much more stubborn. She'd better not weasel out of the bean picking, weaker or not, I thought. Maybe we should have kept our beans separate. Bet that way I'd earn more money than she would. As I thought about the money race I'd win, I felt a sly smile tickle my lips as I washed dishes. My dreams of all the clothes and fabric I'd buy made my head spin with dollars as green as the beans I'd be picking the next day.

I surely was glad about the Stokely's bean factory being in Frederic. In the end, we managed to afford the blue felt and sewed stunning skirts from it. And we got the neon socks.

See Sally Sin

Mom determined to keep us on the straight and narrow by enrolling us in Pilgrim Lutheran's confirmation class. Except during the winter, we often walked to the church where we met every Saturday. Shirley Graf joined us as we walked along the highway the almost two miles to town.

Our class was large. Again, being shy, we listened but kept silent when the pastor asked questions. He was old, nearing retirement, and rigid in his ways. But I absorbed everything he taught. One of the first things I memorized was the 66 books of the Bible. Then we learned the Apostles' Creed, along with its meaning as written by Martin Luther. San and I practiced memorizing while we did our chores, determined to get everything right so we could be confirmed into the Lutheran faith.

Like some of the other girls in our class, we spent too much time giggling. However, the lessons made a deep impression on me. They helped point my moral compass in the godly direction Mom and God both would want for me. But I

179

didn't always adhere to all the commandments I learned in those classes.

In fact, toward fall before the second year of classes began, I deliberately broke the third commandment. It happened as we helped shock grain. As Daddy cut the oats, it fell in bunches along the field. Our job required picking up each swath and making miniature tents of six or eight bunches so they would dry before the threshing crew harvested. Daddy didn't want wet oats in his barn.

Often we shocked the grain with the help of our friend Catha. One day we decided against boredom by pretending to be our dads or our farmer-neighbor, who was noted for being a hard-cussing man. We competed with each other to see who could out-swear the other. I knew it was a sin against God to use His name in vain. With every cuss word I uttered, my heart cried with sorrow while I laughed with Catha and my twin. I vowed never to swear again.

The day of our confirmation into the Lutheran faith brought fear, relief, and happiness. I had spent two years memorizing all the required doctrines plus countless Bible verses. I spent many silent hours meditating on them. They became rote but rich in meaning to my busy mind. But would I remember any of the material while standing in front of the congregation as the pastor asked me questions? My heart pounded with fear.

Later, I felt relief at surviving my anxiety. A smile could have split my face. I felt proud. And happy that God had accepted me into His family.

Mom planned a small celebration following our confirmation. We looked nice in our dresses, special ones that had been purchased rather than handmade. We received a leather-bound Bible from the church and a stunning string of valuable, real pearls from our spinster relative, Great-aunt Eula.

As a new "child of God," I prayed often that I wouldn't sin again. But I did.

One day Mom said she was taking me to the doctor. I had no way of knowing why, as I wasn't sick. San and I rode in the back of Daddy's car to the office where Mom spoke with the doctor. He then ushered me into an examination room. The surprise pelvic exam made me feel humiliated. I had done nothing wrong. How could Mom think I'd had sex with my boyfriend? He'd barely kissed me. In fact, like most other girls in our high school class, I remained a virgin until marriage.

I hated Mom for forcing me to endure such an ordeal. I especially hated her for her silence. That's when I broke the commandment about honoring my parents. It took me years to forgive her in my heart, and only when our sister Jo later told us she had given birth to a child out of wedlock right after her graduation. Then I understood Mom didn't want such a thing to happen in her family again.

Run, Sally, Run Fast

Daddy had joined other neighbor men in hiring a grain-threshing rig. When our turn came, San and I spent hours helping Mom get ready to feed the large crew of workers. We acted as waitresses while the men emptied one large bowl of food after another. I couldn't believe how much they ate. Then, once finished with the meal, they rushed back to the oat field and the barn until afternoon lunch time, while we cleared the table and washed and dried the dishes.

We took our turn eating then began preparing for their lunch. It meant making scary trips down the basement to retrieve Mom's colorful jars of sauces and jams. It meant cutting dozens of extra-thick slices of her homemade bread and resetting the table. We held our breath, hoping all the men would get their fill.

The next day, the crew worked at another farm. Then another. Until one hot, muggy day while Daddy and the crew ate their noon meal at a farm about a mile away, we picked beans at home. We watched storm clouds roll in, wondering if we'd be able to finish a row before the storm hit. Then Mom called us in for our noon meal.

"It's coming fast," Mom said. "Hurry, let's go in to wait it out over lunch."

She helped us dump our pails of beans into a gunny sack. With just the three of us, we ate a quick, light lunch. While a pan of tomato soup heated on the stove, a sharp crackle of lightning followed by an immediate, loud thunderclap made us all jump. The lights went out. Our telephone rang then stopped. The line had been struck again. With all our summer storms, lightning had put our phone out of service several times.

I happened to look out the kitchen window toward the barn. Rain poured down so hard, I could see little. But what I saw made my heart pound. Flames were licking the barn roof.

"The barn's on fire!" I shouted.

None of us dared touch the phone to call the fire department.

"Hurry, kids," Mom yelled. "We have to go to the Taylors'."

We threw jackets over our heads and raced out the back door, but not before I took a quick glance back and turned off the gas range under our pot of tomato soup.

Unrelenting bolts of lightning chased us. Booming thunder followed each ear-shattering crack. As we ran downhill, facing the torrents of rain that drenched us and the wind gusts that threatened to push us back home, I cried. I worried our house would burn, too.

San and I ran way ahead of Mom, our pet collie, Prince, barking and nipping our heels all the way.

At the Taylors' driveway we waited for Mom, gasping for breath. The three of us burst through their door.

"Our barn's on fire," Mom said, breathless and red-faced. "Call the fire department."

One of the Taylor girls cranked their phone, shouted to the operator, and gave our name. "Ed Christiansen's barn," she said, "northeast of Frederic."

Shivering from the cold rain, we waited. And waited. We heard no sirens, even after the storm had passed. A good half hour slipped by before the fire truck arrived.

One of the Taylors finally drove us home, where Daddy stood by the firefighters, who by now could do nothing to save the barn. The fire fighters had mistakenly gone to the other Ed Christiansen farm, the one northwest of town.

We lost three calves that day, a haymow full of new alfalfa, and a place to milk our cows. The barn smoldered all day and through the night. As San and I returned to our bean patch that week, the stench of our dead calves turned our stomachs until someone finally buried them.

After the fire, time and events accelerated.

See Sally Cry

The week before Labor Day, Mom made an announcement.

"Grandpa and Grandma are coming for a visit," she said.

San and I exchanged smiles, happy to be with Grandpa again. But Mom didn't look too happy about it. Not that she didn't love to see her parents, she must have worried about how she'd get all her gardening and canning done while they stayed with us. Grandpa required more care, with his growing memory loss.

The day they arrived on the first day of September brought great change to our household. Neither grandparent could go up and down the stairs, without effort, and Grandpa needed a bathroom nearby. That meant they took over Mom and Daddy's bedroom. And that meant our parents were forced to sleep upstairs.

Daddy didn't like the new arrangement. He never had given much time or effort toward Mom's family. And he must have felt pressured enough. He wanted the new barn built before winter. He had to finish harvesting the crops. He had to travel back and forth to a neighbor's farm to do the milking and feeding of our cows. And now he was being pushed out of his own bed.

Mom didn't smile much those days. Her hands were filled to overflowing. Garden harvest meant hours and days of pulling, preparing, and canning vegetables. She could barely keep up with her household chores of cooking and cleaning, let alone babysitting her parents. And, back in school, San and I could do little to help.

Mom and Daddy argued, always in the privacy of my bedroom. Even while lying in San's bed, the one we always shared, we heard their angry voices through the crack under the bedroom door. Many times we heard Mom crying.

We didn't sleep well. Their arguing continued. Mom cried. Grandpa coughed constantly, which we heard through the heat register on the floor. Grandma got up often to fix a dose of Asthmador. Its strong fumes helped ease Grandpa's asthmatic breathing, but they also wafted up through the register. Not too unpleasant, they still caused my nose to burn.

Mom told us earlier that Grandpa had asthma from all the years he farmed. He didn't smoke, but he did chew Copenhagen snuff. And his poor memory meant he sometimes forgot and spit in places he shouldn't have. It didn't take long for Mom to place saucers and small paper bags around the downstairs rooms to remind Grandpa to use them instead of the floor. I avoided looking at the nasty contents.

As he had done throughout our lives, Grandpa kept looking at our identical faces and asking us how we could tell which one was which. The first few times during their visit, we looked at each other and giggled while he laughed. Soon the ritual grew old. So we tried to stay out of his way.

One Saturday Grandpa wandered into the kitchen where I was helping Mom. She had picked gallons of chokecherries, cooked them down, and strained the seeds. Her huge, ten-gallon boiler full of juice now sat on the stove awaiting jelly jars.

I turned my head just in time to see Grandpa spit into the boiler. My stomach churned. Should I tell Mom? If not, how could I think about anyone eating the jelly? So I told her. She cried. She cried easily those days.

Much as I loved Grandpa and Grandma, I hoped they'd leave soon, to stay with other relatives. Then Mom talked

Grandma into taking Grandpa to a nursing home. The transfer took place twelve days after they had arrived.

Grandpa's admittance to the Grantsburg nursing home did not mean our household returned to normal—nor did it ease the tension between Mom and Daddy. Grandma remained with us. And with Daddy so busy with barn building and farming and reluctance to help Mom, Grandma had little or no chance to visit her dying husband. The stress accelerated. The vegetables ripened. The weather cooled.

Busy as she was, Mom made sure we kept up with our high school homework. We often studied in the enclosed front porch, away from busy-ness and conflict. My thoughts wandered often. I found myself making up stories in my mind. What if Grandpa died and Grandma ended up living with us? What if Mom and Daddy divorced? What if their fights became violent? Story after story overtook my thoughts as I tried to keep my emotions under control.

When we could, San and I helped Mom. Besides doing the weekly cleaning and washing and drying the dishes every evening, we helped with the laundry. Every week, the time-consuming chore meant filling Mom's huge galvanized boiler with water for heating, dipping the hot water out, pail by pail, and toting it to the Maytag wringer-washer. It meant filling the double rinse tubs with cold water. We made trip after trip from kitchen to back porch. It meant placing each item of washed clothing into the wringer without getting our fingers caught. Rinsing each garment up and down in both rinse tubs. Hanging the wash out on the backyard clotheslines. Taking it all down, once dry. Ironing most of the items, including dish towels.

Our help relieved Mom from some of her chores, but not enough. And the day Grandpa died, September 24, 1951, brought little ease. Grandma regressed to being like a child, which meant Mom's work multiplied. She was too busy to grieve her father's death. Of his four daughters, she had grown up closest to him. She had been favored as a child because she exhibited the same interests and temperament as her dad. While living on the North Dakota prairie, Grandpa showed Mom how to fix broken farm equipment and how to splice rope. She sprawled with him on the prairie grass in evenings where he taught her the names of the stars. He taught her how to ride a horse bareback. Of the four girls, she enjoyed the farm the most, and became his helper with the animals and farm work.

Mom loved him and now he was gone. The week between his death and funeral while caring for Grandma lasted a year, in my mind. Among added chores, Mom had to coordinate funeral plans with her three sisters. The funeral took place in Roberts, Illinois, where Grandpa and Grandma had lived and their siblings and parents were buried.

Mom and Grandma took the train to Roberts, where Grandma would stay with other family members after Grandpa's funeral. During Mom's absence, Daddy moved back downstairs. We felt relief that Grandma was gone, but we missed Mom for the few days she spent in Illinois. We took over household chores, which included cooking. Our Home Economics classes paid off—we made tolerable meals for Daddy.

Once back home, Mom returned to her work routine. I hoped their fighting would stop. But it didn't. End-of-the-season chores continued, as did the completion of the new barn. Our farm took on the appearance of a chaotic three-ring circus, with men shouting back and forth, pounding nails and hoisting shingles high onto the new roof. Mom scurried to and from the garden with arms laden with carrots and potatoes. Daddy kept his John Deere busy pulling one tractor attachment after another as he tried to beat the season with his farm work.

Mom looked exhausted. Even with our help, she couldn't keep up with all her work. And when the workmen finished building the barn, tension continued. The situation should have improved. The cows were back in their new stalls, the haymow filled with late crop alfalfa, the corncrib overflowing with dry cobs of corn.

But our parents kept quarreling. Always about money. Or Daddy's drinking. From upstairs in bed, we often heard Mom crying. And mealtimes remained as quiet and stressful as ever. I overate—my way of dealing with the anxiety. San could eat little.

My imagined stories grew. What if Daddy hit Mom? What if she left us forever? What if something happened to Daddy and we were left orphaned? On and on the mental scenarios marched, like an enemy army. Then … one of my stories came true.

On a Saturday morning Mom came upstairs to wake us. We didn't appreciate being wakened on our day off from school. She grabbed my arm and shook it.

"Kids, get up," she said, her voice a stretched wire. "Get dressed. Hurry. Daddy's going to kill me."

"What? No he's not," I yelled, pulling away. Not Daddy, I thought. He didn't have it in him to do such a thing.

Mom insisted. I balked, argued. But both of us finally dressed.

"Hurry," she said. "We have to get to the Taylors' before Daddy finishes chores."

The walk down to the Taylors' became more like a run as we tried to keep up with Mom. She seemed desperate. When we arrived, Mom crying, we kept silent in their kitchen until Catha beckoned us outside where we followed her to the barn, a safe, quiet place. At least for a time.

Events tumbled like pickup sticks later in the day. Daddy drove down to talk. Mrs. Taylor called Mom's sister, Lucille, who came from near Amery with her husband. Then they left with Mom, driving her to a private sanitarium near Prescott, Wisconsin, where she remained for a short while.

Meanwhile, no one told San and me anything. All we knew was Mom was "resting" there and we would be in charge of her household chores. We felt no fear of Daddy, yet the stress of the situation remained. One day he drove us to visit Mom. The building scared me. Patients roamed the halls, hollering to each other and mumbling. Mom lay on a single bed, telling us she hated the place. But fear showed in her eyes. And despair. I wanted to cry.

She did come home soon after our visit. The atmosphere changed a little. Surprising us, Daddy kissed Mom every time he went to the barn. She acted a bit more relaxed. We'd never seen any display of affection between them until the day Mom came home. In fact, we wondered how they ever decided to marry, as mismatched as they seemed. That is, until I learned years later that she had been pregnant with Jo.

Blow, Sally, Blow

Our house became somewhat more relaxed after Mom came home from the sanitarium. And soon after, she took the Greyhound bus to Minneapolis to find a job. She came home on weekends, acted happier. It made us feel happier, even though we were saddled with her household chores during the few weeks she worked.

By now the thunderstorms had stopped but not the rains. Soon it would snow. Then one November day a cold wind began to blow.

An outhouse sat along the fence line about a hundred feet from our house.

Not that we used the outhouse much. It came with the farm, so we left it standing. Actually, it became handy when we had company. Lots of company, that is. Such as during our annual family reunions. Since we had a big, shady yard, reunions at our place became a favorite spot. Especially for Daddy's big family. He had seven brothers and sisters. One sister had ten children. One of her ten children had ten, also. So the cousins flocked to our place along with their folks.

The outhouse got lots of use during those summer events. On that November day in 1951, however, no one visited nor used the outhouse. While the cold wind howled outside, we huddled in the house.

San and I dared not huddle too long, though. The school bus was due soon. We hurried and dressed while standing over our big, square heat register between the two pillars that separate the living and dining rooms.

"Hurry, kids. You don't want to miss the bus," Mom called from the kitchen.

"Why do they have school today, anyway?" I whined. "It looks like it might snow any minute."

It was Friday, Mom's bread baking day. I'd use any excuse to stay home and help her bake that day. I loved her homemade bread.

I made one last, mad dash for the bathroom, glad I didn't have to use the dilapidated outhouse on such a wind-scary day. Mom pursed her lips and practically shoved us out the door, handing each of us a sack lunch. She had other household chores to do before starting on the bread making. And she'd likely be called on to help Daddy in the barn, too. A cow was due to freshen soon. Another excuse to stay home, but Mom didn't rise to my whiny bait.

Once outside, San and I braced ourselves against the wind, pushing hard as we ran along the driveway to the gravel road where the bus picked us up. Puddles from a recent rain filled the holes in the road. The strong wind made tiny waves in the puddles.

The wind, at our backs, blew fiercely across the neighbor's field. We clung to each other, feet braced apart to keep from falling. As the smallest kids in our classroom, Daddy called us lightweights.

The bus arrived. We rode to school and began our classes. The wind grew stronger. It whistled between the window cracks in our old, brick school. During the lunch hour, I kept checking out the window for that first snowflake. But it didn't come. Just spits of rain carried in the wind. *Please, Lord, let it snow.* I tried to remember to pray for things like our pastor had told us in confirmation class. When the wind grew dangerously high, our principal decided to let us out a couple hours early. Yeah! No math class today. Guess the Lord answered my prayer in a different way than I expected. Wasn't that just like Him?

Two hundred school kids poured outside the building to our waiting buses. Br-r! It had grown colder since morning. The rain had become more than a sputtering spit.

Once on the bus, our driver took us down the town's winding hill and along Coon Lake. I'd never seen the water so high. It scared me. When the driver slowed the bus to a crawl, everyone crowded to the left side to peer out the windows. Some of us gasped. Not so much from the bus rocking off-balance, but from seeing lake water blow across the road in waves. The wind shoved one wave onto the next until it looked like a miniature waterfall.

Luckily, the depth of water on the road wasn't enough to stop the bus. Our driver remained cautious, though, and we collectively held our breath as he guided us through.

I couldn't wait to get home. What if we had more "floods" to go through? What if it started to snow? What if a tree blew down and hit the bus? I saw fear in San's eyes, too. Everyone remained quiet as the bus driver stopped along his route to let kids off at their homes.

We finally reached our road. Just as I feared, water filled the road at the bottom of Taylors' hill. Would we make it through? At other times, the road had been closed because of high water.

Again, the driver slowed to a crawl but made it through. I sighed with relief. Almost home now.

Up the long, sloped hill we went until we reached our driveway where the bus driver said goodbye and, as usual, told us to be careful. As we stepped off the bus, the wind nearly tore our scarves from our heads. It was always windy on our hill. Mom claimed it to be one of the highest spots in Wisconsin.

Usually I liked the wind. But not today. Today it didn't show itself as mischievous, soothing, or cooling as it usually did. Today it became a rock-solid force to avoid.

But it couldn't be avoided while we ran along our driveway. It pushed us sideways until we stumbled, stopped, stumbled, stopped. *Please don't let our trees fall on us,* I prayed. And they didn't. We made it to the house safely.

Inside, I threw my coat on a chair, flung my scarf off, and inhaled the heavenly scent of Mom's homemade bread. Safe inside, I felt nothing could touch me. Safe from the brutal wind that kept howling outside. Safe from falling trees. Safe from the banshee-like wind.

As I savored a slice of Mom's still-warm bread slathered with butter and her raspberry jam, I watched out the back porch window. The new, sturdy barn stood, its resident Holstein and Guernsey cows and calves, and the resident cats, safe from the battering gale. The little, slant-roofed chicken house down the hill by the well pit lay safely tucked among a small forest of shrubs. The outhouse by the fence line stood … rocked … teetered ….

"Look," I shouted, my mouth full of bread. "The outhouse!"

Mom and Daddy and San came running—just in time to watch the outhouse topple, end over end, across the back yard toward the barn.

We ran to the north window. There, from the bowels of the outhouse now lying in a heap of sticks by the corn crib, a blizzard of toilet paper streamers unwound. They caught on tree limbs. They floated high in the air. They moved at a dizzying speed, festooning the farmyard like hilltop beacons, shouting to our cousins and other kin to stay home until next summer. We had to build a new outhouse first.

I prayed. *Thank You, Lord, for indoor plumbing.*

Ride, Sally, Ride

The next two-and-a-half years of high school became a blur. With somewhat less stress at home and with routine set in place, San and I focused on learning, working, and preparing for future careers.

Several events pulled us out of our routine, the most exciting which was Jo's wedding. She and Lorry Hjulberg, after several years of dating, were married in his parents' Lutheran church in Oak Knoll, Minnesota, a suburb of Minneapolis. Jo chose five bridesmaids, including San and me. She made all five of our dresses out of aqua satin covered with netting of the same color. She made wide-brimmed, lacy hats, and elbow-length, fingerless net gloves.

We anticipated the wedding for weeks. Jo made several trips to the farm for dress fittings. We loved the times she visited. Her presence helped us relax. She and Mom stayed up late each night, sitting at the dining room table where they told jokes and laughed for hours. San and I sneaked down the five steps to the landing where we sat to listen. Mom must have known of our presence, for they made sure we couldn't hear the jokes.

Years earlier, Daddy had traded his Chevy for a stick-shift pickup. So when time came to drive to Oak Knoll for the wedding, we rode in the open back. Daddy swept it clean for us. Mom made us promise to sit with our backs against the cab. Our excitement over-rode the discomfort as we sang song after song to pass the time. Our normally soft voices, now uninhibited, rode with the wind that day.

The time spent dressing and practicing our walk down the aisle and meeting all of Jo's friends became a blur. Mom argued with Jo because she didn't want to wear a bra.

"I've never worn a bra in my life," she said, "and I never will." And she didn't.

We met the best-man and four groomsmen, Lorry's tall, dark, handsome friends. Lorry's short, smiley mother giggled and talked with her friends in their native Finnish language as they watched us "twinnies."

The event remained in our dreams for days, but life went on. Back home, we drove Daddy's John Deere as he harvested the late crop of hay. We attended Sunday school and church with our friends each weekend. We rode with them to the Lewis roller skating rink, eyeing each new boy we saw, waiting to be asked for a round of skating.

Sometimes I rode with my friend, Joanne, in her Model A Ford. One night it began to rain, meaning I had to move the internally-controlled windshield wipers back and forth manually. One time we had to push her old car uphill when it stalled. But we never let such inconveniences stop us from having fun when we could.

We looked forward to the time when we could drive, so before our senior year San and I signed up for Driver's Training classes, taught by the high school shop teacher. We agreed everything was easy to learn except parallel parking. Through practice, we passed.

Back home, we drove Daddy's pickup. Nothing was easy about it. Without power steering, we struggled to turn the wheel. Without automatic drive, we struggled to keep the engine from dying and the truck from rolling backwards before being able to change gears. San's best friend lived down our road and across the state highway. The intersection was on a blind curve. Mom, ever concerned for our safety, insisted on going along with us to visit San's friend. At the crossing, she got out of the pickup, walked across the highway, and when she believed it safe enough, beckoned us across.

We did little driving but felt proud to carry our own driver's licenses.

See Sally Vote

I also awaited the day I would be able to vote. No license was needed, only my signature and address. And if I couldn't vote for president at the local precinct booth, I could vote at school. Early in our junior year, the Social Studies class received the distinct privilege to cast our ballots in a mock election on the first Tuesday of November, 1952. After learning all about the presidential candidates, I decided to vote for Republican Dwight David Eisenhower. Daddy had been a Democrat all his life. But I liked what I read about Ike. He was the most famous U.S. Army general of WWII. His leadership had helped us win the war against the Germans in Europe, especially in France, according to reports.

I felt doubly proud to have cast my vote when "Ike" won the presidency over Robert Taft. Ike ran again four years later, over Adlai Stevenson, when I had reached the age of voting that counted. During Ike's presidency, our nation enjoyed relative peace and prosperity in spite of the Cold War with the Soviet Union and China.

Walk, Sally, Walk

That summer and the previous, San and I applied for jobs at Stokely's cannery located on the outer edge of Frederic. Our friend, Catha, also signed up, and during the green bean season we were hired to work the second shift. It meant walking the two miles to town each afternoon, working at the assembly line removing cans of beans from huge buckets onto the moving line for labeling. It meant standing on our feet from four o'clock till midnight then walking home.

Frederic became a ghost town at night. We saw almost no cars along the main street, the only light coming from the lampposts at each corner. The six blocks we walked to our first turn found us laughing and sharing how we'd spend our paychecks. At the turn, we lost all light unless a moon shone down from above. Even then, walking along the thick woods on either side of the road meant little light. Back then, before houses had been built past the high school, kids avoided those woods even in daylight.

Yet another quarter mile before the next turn found us hurrying. We knew the worst loomed ahead. And yet another quarter mile before our final turn meant we hardly spoke, breathless in our speed walking. We ran past Hoosier's woods of sugar maples, dodged the shadows near Eklofs' place, and slowed our steps as we approached the looming Haunted House.

The ramshackle building sat back into the woods, unused for years and surrounded by weeds and tall grass. By daylight it appeared as a non-threatening, old hut that had been abandoned. But rumors circulated, whether true or not, that it was haunted. And when the wind blew, eerie sounds brought shivers to every passerby. So we slowed our steps, listening for perceived danger before we turned the corner. Then we ran past as if a pack of wolves chased us. Down the hill we ran, stumbling, until we slowed at Catha's driveway.

Once there, San and I had another quarter mile to walk to our own house. The way should have been easy, with no woods on either side of the road. But we still begged Catha to walk at least part way with us. And she did, without fail. She was our angel during those nights.

In spite of our fear of the dark and of the hard work, we smiled with every paycheck that we could spend on school clothes. By September we had bought and sewn enough to outfit us for the coming school year. How blessed we were.

See Sally Type

What vocation should I choose after high school graduation? I wondered. I had already decided not to pursue the careers of dietetics and teaching. Each meant that I'd be required to take classes in mathematics. It scared me off, so I opted for the field of stenography. I took every class the school offered. Typing. Shorthand. Office Practice, which included learning how to file papers. Even Bookkeeping.

I enjoyed the classes. By the time I finished learning how to type without errors, on the Smith-Corona typewriter with its replaceable ribbon, I could type 120 words a minute. And shorthand, by the Gregg method, became my favorite class. Like learning a new language, I dreamed in shorthand, wrote my class notes in shorthand, and wrapped my thoughts around shorthand. Again, I excelled in the class.

But I kept pursuing fun with my friends. Not all of our activities turned out to be fun, however. Before school ended during our junior year, I encountered a couple unpleasant experiences with boys. One day my friend, Joanne, who had quit school and was engaged to a soldier, asked if San and I wanted to go for a ride with them and her soldier's friends. She also invited one other girl.

We left in the fiance's car, the eight of us so crowded that except for Joanne, we girls had to sit on the boys' laps. We didn't know the guys, nor did we drink beer as they did during our country jaunt. And we had a curfew, which we couldn't control. San and I were scared. We refused to take a walk with our "partner," and refused to drink. Our classmate did, however, and they walked into the woods where they stayed for a long time. Meanwhile, we sat waiting, taking turns begging the driver to take us home.

Finally he honked his horn so the walking couple would hurry back, and we got home just ahead of our curfew, with great relief. The next day in school, our classmate bragged to all the girls that she had lost her virginity that night. The news shocked many of us. How close had San and I been to being molested? A sense of relief and thanksgiving to God overwhelmed me.

The other incident happened one very cold night during our senior year. San was dating Wally, her future husband, who attended college in River Falls. One weekend he came home for a visit, bringing a friend with him so we could double date. We went out for a meal and then parked in our driveway to talk. San and Wally sat in the front seat talking and kissing, while I sat in the back trying to deflect my date's roaming hands.

San and I finally went inside and climbed the stairs to go to bed. Next thing we knew, we heard a knock at the back door. Daddy got out of bed to let Wally and his friend in. Once inside the porch, Wally fainted. Mom and Daddy got them inside, where they lay Wally on the couch and managed to revive him. It seems his car tires had locked from the severe cold before they left our driveway. While working on the car, Wally's lungs had frozen from breathing the air. The thermometer read about 40 degrees below zero. We had been foolish to go out at all that night.

Upstairs, San and I fretted and giggled, knowing the guys were sleeping in the living room overnight, wondering what we'd do if we had to use the downstairs bathroom. And I wondered if my date would try to come upstairs and finish his groping of my body.

Again, I felt relief and gratitude to God when the night ended.

Run, Sally, Run to New Beginnings

Graduation day. A move to the Twin Cities. A new career.

Overwhelmed by the fast pace, I bounced from excitement to fear. Where would I live and work? Would I even be hired for a full-time secretarial job? What kind of boss would I have? And how much money would I make? My biggest fear, how would it feel to be separated from San every day?

Doubts about my abilities plagued me. The constricting routine of school and home suddenly seemed like Utopia. I sent little arrow prayers to God, asking Him for success, for peace of mind.

But first, graduation day. An exciting time for us and our friends. A sense of relief having made it through twelve years of study without failing. We had already written in each others' yearbook, *The Magnet.*

"You and Sandra are always up to something," one classmate wrote. "Be good," another scrawled across his picture.

Some wrote words of encouragement. "Keep doing the good work

... and you will go far," a boy wrote. Another wrote a cryptic message: "Did you learn anything this year? I think I learned enough for a few years."

Under each picture of graduating students was a short quote. Mine read, "Here's a young lady as good as gold, not too shy, not too bold." I saw myself as *too* shy and *not* bold, but in time that changed.

The quote under San's photo made me feel jealous. "She smiled and you couldn't help but like her." I always had been envious of her Pepsodent smile.

The personal message she wrote in my yearbook beside her picture made me laugh. "Dear sis, since we know each other's business, I might as well not rite much 'cuz there's nothin' to say. Lotsa luck to a dear sweet sister, love, 'San.'"

That year's ceremony would start a new trend—scheduling it on a Sunday. My friend and the valedictorian of our class belonged to the Seventh-day Adventist church, so a Saturday ceremony didn't fit with her church's beliefs. And as a challenge to the weather, our class decided to hold it on the football field.

Our parents attended, of course, helping to fill the bleachers on our special day. It passed in a blur, and before we knew it we were job hunting. Since Daddy took the Sunday Minneapolis Star and Tribune, we perused the want-ads for weeks before our graduation. With Mom's help, we also sought a good, cheap, safe place to live. We applied for jobs and waited.

Once we received letters asking us to be interviewed, Mom took the Greyhound with us and helped set us up, with two of our friends, at a girls' club near the St. Paul cathedral. Our rent included board and room so the only other expense we had was our lunches.

See Sally in St. Paul

Our new freedom set our hearts pounding.
The day had come when we shed all of
Mom's household and social rules. We
could do as we pleased. No more
boundaries. Not that we changed our safe,
staid lifestyle, for young girls of our ilk kept
their "good girl" reputation all their lives.
But the difference came in being away from
Mom. We now were ready to listen to
someone else's rules of conduct.

Sandy's first job was at a downtown
bank. I took a job at the St. Paul Fire &
Marine Insurance Company. With my first
paycheck I bought a set of yellow, ceramic
swans for Mom's dining room table. I stayed
at my job a few months but the routine
bored me and kept me from using my talents
as a secretary.

Soon after, I applied for a steno job
with the Minnesota Department of
Education, a job I loved. And working away
from San didn't bother me as much as I
expected. We roomed together at the girl's
club and hung out with the same friends so
kept in close contact. Most weekends we
either took a bus home or stayed in the

Cities with our friends. We walked everywhere. On nice days we walked to the Mississippi river or along Summit Avenue where we eyed the beautiful mansions built in the 1800s. Once we walked to a ballroom on University Avenue about five miles away. by the time we arrived, we were too tired to dance.

I had always wanted to learn how to swim, so during that year I signed up for lessons at the downtown YWCA. What an experience!

One of about a dozen other girls, I kept to the edge of the pool. My fear of drowning must have been evident to all of them, including our instructor. In the shallow end, we learned how to float with our heads under water. I managed the maneuver only because we remained at the shallow end. From there we learned various swimming strokes. I mastered the crawl, the butterfly, the dog paddle, and a few other techniques—all while swimming tight against the edge. But when it came to learning how to tread water, my body refused. So I remained at the edge.

The next lesson? Diving from the board. Could I dive to the bottom of the pool, swim to the top and then to the edge? I watched everyone else try. No one floundered. Some dives were awkward but all succeeded in not drowning. If they could do it, so could I.

I practiced in my mind for days. When my turn came, I walked the plank with confidence—at least with visible confidence—then dove. My heart beat like a jackhammer. I stood at the plank's edge, swallowed hard, spread my arms out, and dove. Down I went like a rag doll. Up I came like a geyser. I panicked. Unable to tread water, I went down again. Up I came, gasping. That's the moment I saw it. An eight-foot pole stretched toward me. Like a drowning sailor, I grabbed it. The instructor pulled me to the edge. I never went swimming in deep water again.

I may have been afraid of deep water, but I wasn't afraid to fly. When the opportunity came to help open up the Minnesota Department of Education's FFA camp near Ely for the summer, I took it. Not only would it get me out of the office for a week, I'd be able to enjoy nature at its best in northern lake country.

The man in charge of the State's program flew his own float plane from the small St. Paul airport to the lake up north. I could have fainted from the excitement. As he piloted the single engine plane, he described all the switches and knobs and buttons. The plane had two control sticks, one in front of the pilot and one in front of the co-pilot or, in my case, the passenger.

Halfway to Ely, he surprised me.

"Want to take the controls?"

I nodded, eager to try. I pulled the stick forward to go higher then back to decline. He cautioned me to make slow moves, to avoid flipping over. I moved the stick to the right and felt the plane bank to the east. To the left it banked to the west.

Wait until I could tell San! Her face would turn green with envy.

During my tenure with the State, I piloted—or drove—another vehicle. One weekend Jo and Lorry asked us to babysit their son Gary at their Minneapolis suburban home. We'd never babysat and had little to do with babies, but of course we agreed. Lorry picked us up at the girls' club and drove us most of the way to their house before stopping.

"Why don't you drive, Sal?" He got out of the car to exchange seats before I had a chance to say, "No, I can't, not in the city."

I'd barely driven a block before cutting off another vehicle. It was enough for Lorry to take back the wheel. I didn't drive again for several years.

One Friday before Christmas that first year, we planned to ride home with our friend's brother. He would meet us at the girl's club at a certain time. Meanwhile, after work I hurried to Dayton's to pick up a gift to take home for Mom. The gift, a floor lamp, weighed a ton but I managed to haul it uphill to the girls' club. The solid brass base, unlike later lamps made of lighter metal, made my arms ache for days. But how happy and proud I felt giving it to Mom that Christmas weekend, knowing I had bought it with my own money.

Before that Christmas when I was still seventeen, my Seventh-day Adventist friend introduced me to her church and one of the families she hung out with who lived a few blocks away from our girls' club. I became friends and visited them often. Their strong sense of family and community attracted me, so I began to go to church with them. Through the teachings I learned, I became a true believer in God. It changed my life and I was ready to join their church.

Mom rebelled. She grabbed a bus to St. Paul, told the men who mentored me to leave me alone, and forced me to give up my "foolishness." She talked me into returning to the Lutheran church. But I felt an increasing hunger to know God better, to grow in my new-found faith. Lutheranism may have differed in some theological points, but it did teach salvation by faith in Jesus Christ. So I returned to my family's Lutheran roots.

While visiting a local church, I learned about the Lutheran Bible Institute (LBI) in Minneapolis. I checked into it, deciding it was what I needed to grow in the wisdom of the Lord. I enrolled in LBI's two-year Parish Work course, signed up for the work-study program, and quit my lovely job. It meant my income would drop to a pittance, but my "spiritual income" would soar.

San didn't want to sever our ties as identical twin soulmates, so she joined me in our new adventure. One more year together suited me fine. And because my faith meant more to me than running to stay ahead of my twin, I became less competitive with her. I exchanged my feelings of dependence from her to God.

Thus began another chapter of my life, now as a Christian dedicated to following His will in every way possible.

About the Author

Sally Bair has written numerous books. Her first three, for children and adults, are part of her "Ways of the Williwaw" series: *Williwaw Winds, Trouble at Fish Camp,* and *Runaways.*

Another series, taken from her weekly devotional column, "Eternal Perspectives," is called *The Nature of God.* Each of the four is seasonal and includes 91 daily devotionals.

A former journalist and published free-lance writer, Sally has won several awards for her stories. She enjoys inspiring others through speaking engagements and her frequent classes on "Writing Your Life Stories." She enjoys reading, writing, and communing with nature.

Sally has three children, nine grand-kids, and four greats. She makes her home in Wisconsin near the south shore of Lake Superior.

**Run Sally Run
and Sally's other books are
available at**

www.sallybair.com
www.amazon.com

Cedar Haven Books
P.O. Box 186
Washburn WI 54891

Contact sallybair@gmail.com
for further information